THE PRESIDENT'S IRAN DECISION: NEXT STEPS

HEARING

BEFORE THE

SUBCOMMITTEE ON
THE MIDDLE EAST AND NORTH AFRICA

OF THE

COMMITTEE ON FOREIGN AFFAIRS
HOUSE OF REPRESENTATIVES

ONE HUNDRED FIFTEENTH CONGRESS

FIRST SESSION

OCTOBER 25, 2017

Serial No. 115–77

Printed for the use of the Committee on Foreign Affairs

Available via the World Wide Web: http://www.foreignaffairs.house.gov/ or
http://www.gpo.gov/fdsys/

U.S. GOVERNMENT PUBLISHING OFFICE

27–285PDF   WASHINGTON : 2017

For sale by the Superintendent of Documents, U.S. Government Publishing Office
Internet: bookstore.gpo.gov   Phone: toll free (866) 512–1800; DC area (202) 512–1800
Fax: (202) 512–2104   Mail: Stop IDCC, Washington, DC 20402–0001

COMMITTEE ON FOREIGN AFFAIRS

EDWARD R. ROYCE, California, *Chairman*

CHRISTOPHER H. SMITH, New Jersey
ILEANA ROS-LEHTINEN, Florida
DANA ROHRABACHER, California
STEVE CHABOT, Ohio
JOE WILSON, South Carolina
MICHAEL T. McCAUL, Texas
TED POE, Texas
DARRELL E. ISSA, California
TOM MARINO, Pennsylvania
MO BROOKS, Alabama PAUL
COOK, California SCOTT
PERRY, Pennsylvania RON
DeSANTIS, Florida
MARK MEADOWS, North Carolina
TED S. YOHO, Florida
ADAM KINZINGER, Illinois
LEE M. ZELDIN, New York
DANIEL M. DONOVAN, Jr., New York
F. JAMES SENSENBRENNER, Jr.,
  Wisconsin
ANN WAGNER, Missouri
BRIAN J. MAST, Florida
FRANCIS ROONEY, Florida
BRIAN K. FITZPATRICK, Pennsylvania
THOMAS A. GARRETT, Jr., Virginia
Vacant

ELIOT L. ENGEL, New York
BRAD SHERMAN, California
GREGORY W. MEEKS, New York
ALBIO SIRES, New Jersey
GERALD E. CONNOLLY, Virginia
THEODORE E. DEUTCH, Florida
KAREN BASS, California
WILLIAM R. KEATING, Massachusetts
DAVID N. CICILLINE, Rhode Island
AMI BERA, California
LOIS FRANKEL, Florida
TULSI GABBARD, Hawaii
JOAQUIN CASTRO, Texas
ROBIN L. KELLY, Illinois
BRENDAN F. BOYLE, Pennsylvania
DINA TITUS, Nevada
NORMA J. TORRES, California
BRADLEY SCOTT SCHNEIDER, Illinois
THOMAS R. SUOZZI, New York
ADRIANO ESPAILLAT, New York
TED LIEU, California

Amy Porter, *Chief of Staff*   Thomas Sheehy, *Staff Director*
Jason Steinbaum, *Democratic Staff Director*

———

Subcommittee on the Middle East and North Africa

ILEANA ROS-LEHTINEN, Florida, *Chairman*

STEVE CHABOT, Ohio
DARRELL E. ISSA, California
RON DeSANTIS, Florida
MARK MEADOWS, North Carolina
PAUL COOK, California
ADAM KINZINGER, Illinois
LEE M. ZELDIN, New York
DANIEL M. DONOVAN, Jr., New York
ANN WAGNER, Missouri
BRIAN J. MAST, Florida
BRIAN K. FITZPATRICK, Pennsylvania

THEODORE E. DEUTCH, Florida
GERALD E. CONNOLLY, Virginia
DAVID N. CICILLINE, Rhode Island
LOIS FRANKEL, Florida
BRENDAN F. BOYLE, Pennsylvania
TULSI GABBARD, Hawaii
BRADLEY SCOTT SCHNEIDER, Illinois
THOMAS R. SUOZZI, New York
TED LIEU, California

CONTENTS

Page

WITNESSES

LETTERS, STATEMENTS, ETC., SUBMITTED FOR THE HEARING

APPENDIX

THE PRESIDENT'S IRAN DECISION: NEXT STEPS

House of Representatives,
Subcommittee on the Middle East and North Africa,
Committee on Foreign Affairs,
Washington, DC.

The subcommittee met, pursuant to notice, at 10:05 a.m., in room 2172 Rayburn House Office Building, Hon. Ileana Ros-Lehtinen (chairman of the subcommittee) presiding.

Ms. Ros-Lehtinen. The subcommittee will come to order.

After recognizing myself and Ranking Member Deutch for our opening statements, I will, then, recognize other members seeking recognition for 1 minute. We will, then, hear from our witnesses. And without objection, witnesses, your prepared statements will be made a part of the record, and members may have 5 days to insert statements and questions for the record, subject to the length limitation and the rules.

Before we begin, I would like to welcome some distinguished guests in the audience. They are here from Israel and are taking part in the State Department's International Visitor Leadership Program. There you go in the back row. Coincidentally, they happen to be here this week as the subcommittee takes its first look at the Iran nuclear deal since President Trump made his announcement last week. We know this is an issue of great importance for our ally Israel, and this subcommittee, this committee, and, indeed, Congress understands the gravity of the situation for Israel, for the United States, for our friends and allies.

So, with that, the chair now recognizes herself for such time as I may consume.

Less than 2 weeks ago, President Trump announced that he would not certify the Iran deal under the requirements of the Iran Nuclear Agreement Review Act. All signs leading up to the certification deadline pointed to decertification. In a speech on U.S. policy toward Iran last month, Ambassador Haley laid out the pillars to be considered when determining Iranian compliance with the nuclear deal, the JCPOA itself, the U.N. Security Council Resolution 2231, and the Iran Nuclear Agreement Review Act.

And I think that this is an important distinction because I know we are going to hear about Iran's technical compliance so that the IAEA and the other P 5+1 continue to believe that Iran is in compliance. So, how can the President decertify, they ask. Well, even if Iran was in full compliance with the JCPOA, which we know isn't the actual case, Iran has flouted the ballistic missile provisions of the U.N. Security Council Resolution 2231, and Iran's continued provocations underscore that the current status quo is not in the national security interest of the United States.

We have to take a look at the totality of the threats and the current situation, work within the framework that we have, and use the tools we have at our disposal. Let us remember that the President, through his obligation from the Iran Nuclear Agreement Review Act, decided that he could not certify whether the suspension of sanctions related to Iran is appropriate and proportionate to the specific and verifiable measures taken by Iran with respect to terminating its illicit nuclear program.

So, when the President announced that he would not certify, but remain in the deal for now while allowing for the opportunity to address its flaws, to strengthen it, I supported that decision. I think it is a sound strategic decision that allows us an opportunity to address some of the concerns we have with our allies, like the lack of EU designations against Iran for non-nuclear-related illicit activity.

It gives us an opportunity to correct the record and get some of the promises and assurances that were given to Congress that haven't actually come to fruition, like when Secretary Kerry testified to Congress that Iran would be subject to "24/7 inspections" and day-to-day accountability. Or when he testified that "When it comes to verification and monitoring, there is absolutely no sunset in this agreement, not in 10 years, not in 15 years, not in 20 years, not in 25 years, no sunset ever." Or when we were told that "For the life of this agreement, however long Iran stays in the NPT and is living up to its obligations, they must live up to the Additional Protocol."

But, as we now know, we don't really have 24/7 anywhere anytime access, especially when it comes to military sites where we haven't even had any access at all. And we know that there are sunset provisions all throughout the deal, and there are dangerous sunset provisions in Resolution 2231, like the sunsets on the conventional military and missile embargoes, which will more than certainly make the region even more dangerous.

We already see Iran sending support and arms to the Houthis, Hezbollah, Hamas, and others. Imagine what we will see when Iran has no restrictions on its ability to acquire conventional weapons or its ability to expand its missile program.

We were also promised that Iran's non-nuclear-related activity would be addressed. Yet, despite assurances from Secretary Kerry after the JCPOA was agreed to, we have not seen a single designation from the EU on Iran since the JCPOA. Think about that. No new designations, no new sanctions, despite Iran's continued support for terror, its ballistic missile testing, and its abysmal human rights record. There was no threat of decertification from the United States for the first several rounds of certifications. Yet, there was no EU activity on Iran's other illicit activity. On the contrary, there were billions and billions of dollars in business agreements signed during that period. And I think now, while the President has decertified, this is precisely the opportunity to get together with our allies and see how we can get them back onboard on holding Iran accountable for its malign activities.

This also gives us an opportunity to raise the bar and do what we should have done in the first place, guarantee that Iran can never become a nuclear weapon state, because, as I said from the very beginning, the deal sets such low benchmarks for Iran that it would be crazy for them not to comply with it, even though it has violated and bent and twisted the deal just to see how far it can go.

Producing excess heavy water only to be bailed out by the U.S. and Russia, building and operating more advanced centrifuges than it should be allowed to operate, these are just some examples that we know about. With Iran, it would be safe to assume that there are other potential violations, like potential violations of Section T. But our P5+1 partners are right; this isn't just a U.S. unilateral issue. There are many, many interested parties.

Unfortunately, some parties, like Russia, are intent on protecting its rogue allies and doing what it can to block any efforts to hold them accountable. Russia has already made it clear that it will not support giving access to Iran's military sites for verification of Section T. I wonder why. We just saw Russia veto a resolution at the U.N. Security Council that would have extended the investigation by international inspectors to determine those responsible for the chemical weapons attack in Syria.

So, how do we address this in a way to ensure that the Iranian threat is contained? As we move forward, we must address what is best for our national security interest, the security of our friend and ally Israel, our allies in the Gulf, and the safety and security of the whole region. These are the very same allies who would be most directly impacted by a nuclear Iran, and they are the ones that have publicly expressed support for this administration's willingness to take our Iran policy in a new direction, one that addresses all of Iran's other illicit activities. We can't address Iran's threat without addressing the totality of the situation, and that is what we are here to do today.

And with that, I am pleased and honored to recognize the ranking member, Mr. Ted Deutch of Florida.

Mr. DEUTCH. Thank you, Madam Chairman. Thanks for convening today's important hearing, and thanks to our witnesses for joining us.

I would also like to acknowledge our friends from Israel who are here as part of the State Department's International Visitor Leadership Program, as we discuss an issue that is so important to the security of both of our nations.

Two days ago we marked an anniversary. It is the type of anniversary, though, that we don't celebrate, but we mourn, because on October 23rd in 1983 two Hezbollah suicide bombers blew themselves up at the Marine barracks in Beirut, killing over 300 American and French servicemembers, peacekeepers, and civilians. This attack, like so many of Hezbollah's deadly terrorist activities over the past several decades, was sponsored and directed by Iran. And while the United States has since built memorials honoring the victims of that attack, Tehran builds a monument honoring the martyrs who perpetrated the attack.

When the President gave his much-anticipated Iran strategies speech 2 weeks ago, he rightly reminded the American people about the nature of the Iranian regime, a regime that took control during the Islamic revolution in 1979 by attacking our Embassy and taking dozens of American citizens and diplomats hostage for 444 days. It is a regime that, since that time, has sought to spread its revolution through proxy militias and terror groups like Hezbollah, a regime that was directly responsible for killing and maiming American soldiers in Iraq, a regime that calls America "the Great Satan," calls Israel "the Little Satan," supports and equips terror groups trying to wipe Israel off the map.

It is a regime that saw Syrian President Bashar Assad torturing and murdering his citizens and sent Hezbollah and the Revolutionary Guard Corps to help him. Half a million Syrians are now dead, with millions forced to flee their homes and their country. A regime that today is stoking unrest in countries across the region to spread its influence through Iraq, Syria, Lebanon, and the Gulf. And this is a regime that in 2009, when Iranian citizens took to the streets to protest election results in a system that is anything but free, responded with a brutal crackdown, including the since famous YouTube video of Iranian college student Neda Agha-Soltan being killed in the street.

Human rights violations, exporting terrorism, threatening us and our allies. That is why, when we saw Iran building a secret and illicit nuclear weapons program, the United States and the world rightly became gravely concerned. It is a terrifying thought to imagine this same regime with control of nuclear weapons.

Now I don't want to relitigate the Iran nuclear deal. I voted against the JCPOA. But we must focus now on the most effective way to counter the Iranian threat in today's reality. The President spoke of working with our allies to counter Iran's malign activities, to impose punishing sanctions outside the nuclear deal, to counter the proliferation of missiles and weapons, and to deny the regime all paths to a nuclear weapon.

While the President was right to give important context on Iran's continued threats and to lay out an overarching strategy, I have been clear that I believe that the President, in threatening to walk away from the deal, will make it harder for us to achieve the changes that we need in policy to strengthen our efforts to combat Iran's dangerous behavior, not because my views of the deal have changed, but because if we are to tackle Iran's dangerous activities, we must be in a position to lead the world to do it.

This whole debate has become a distraction. We should be shoring up support from our allies to go after Iran's malign activities, activity that was never a part of the JCPOA. The chairman of the Joint Chiefs, in testifying in the Senate last month, said, "Iran is adhering to the JCPOA obligations. The JCPOA has delayed Iran's development of nuclear weapons." But he also said that Iran has not changed its malign activity in the region since the JCPOA was signed.

It is precisely that activity that we must aggressively target. The truth is, I know that everyone in this room agrees with the overarching goal. We agree that we cannot allow Iran to develop a nuclear weapon, and we know that they cannot be trusted, so we have to maintain intrusive inspections to ensure compliance. We all understand the need to push back against their support for terror and ongoing military expansion of the region, and we all painfully know that more must be done to bring home Americans who are being cruelly and unjustly held in Iran, including my constituent Bob Levinson.

And as we look specifically to the JCPOA, I think it is important to understand why the President's top national security advisors have cautioned against walking away from the deal. Unilaterally abandoning the nuclear deal without clear cause would leave the United States isolated and make it impossible to do exactly what the President says that we must, lead the other nations in the world, lead our allies to counter Iran.

As Congress debates next steps, I hope that the President will honor his word to work closely with Congress and our allies. The simple truth is that we here in this body cannot simply and unilaterally change an internationally-negotiated agreement. That does not mean, however, that we cannot make progress. This administration and this Congress can and should work with our allies to enforce the restrictions on Iran that exist under the JCPOA, to support the IAEA's ability to verify Iran in compliance, and to crack down on all of Iran's malign activities in the region outside of the JCPOA.

The fact that so many of the critical restrictions on Iran's nuclear program will begin to expire in the coming years should give us pause for concern. The Iranian regime cannot be trusted with an industrial-size nuclear enrichment program which could become possible when the sunsets hit, but we can make firm our commitment to preventing the emergence of an Iranian threshold nuclear state while also honoring our commitments under the JCPOA.

And finally, if this President means what he says about working with Congress, I hope that he will send his national security team to meet with me and the other Democrats on this committee who are committed to addressing Iran's dangerous behavior. Countering Iran has long been a bipartisan issue here on the Hill. Let's not allow this current political environment to undermine that. The stakes are simply too high.

And I yield back.

Ms. ROS-LEHTINEN. Thank you so much, Mr. Deutch.

And I have the following members who I will recognize for 1 minute. If you would like to be added, please let us know. It is Mr. DeSantis, then Mr. Cicilline, and Mr. Schneider.

So, Mr. DeSantis is recognized.

Mr. DESANTIS. Well, I thank my friend from Florida for holding this hearing. It is important.

I think it is pretty clear, after living under this deal, that if we continue on this course with Iran, 5 or 10 years down the road we are going to be in the same place that we are with North Korea right now, only this is a regime motivated by a militant Islamic ideology and an apocalyptic worldview. So, simply status quo I don't think is going to work.

I note that, for talks about Iranian violations, which they have done, some people try to say that this has been very successful. The fact is we don't have access to all of their sites. You can't go into their military site and inspect their military facilities. So, the idea that we know what Iran has been up to, we don't. It is not an effective regime. They frontloaded all the benefits to Iran at the outset, and it is not something that is going to lead to a permanently disarmed Iran. So, let's fix it. Let's get it right. And I appreciate the President's decertification, but that is just the first step and we need to do a lot more.

I yield back.

Ms. ROS-LEHTINEN. Thank you very much, Mr. DeSantis.

Mr. Cicilline is recognized.

Mr. CICILLINE. Thank you, Madam Chairman. I want to thank you and Ranking Member Deutch for this important hearing.

I would like to welcome our Israeli friends who are visiting us here today.

And, of course, welcome to our distinguished panel, and I look forward to hearing from all of you.

One of the most powerful arguments that was made in support of the agreement to prevent Iran from being a nuclear weapon state is that it will strengthen our ability to respond aggressively and effectively to the malign and increasingly aggressive behavior of this regime, and at the same time will fortify our partnerships and alliances around the world that are really essential to doing this successfully.

And so, in that spirit, I am very, very concerned about the President's lack of leadership on this in terms of simply refusing to certify it without any basis for that, creating great uncertainty and undermining, frankly, our ability to effectively work with our partners in the region to respond to the ongoing malignant activities of Iran. And so, I will conclude by associating myself with the very thoughtful remarks of my distinguished colleague from Florida, Mr. Deutch.

With that, I yield back.

Ms. ROS-LEHTINEN. Thank you, Mr. Cicilline.

Mr. Schneider.

Mr. SCHNEIDER. Thank you, Chairman. Thank you for convening this meeting.

And as my colleague from Rhode Island, I will associate myself with the remarks from our colleague from Florida. I thought they were wonderful.

I want to welcome our witnesses. Thank you for joining us.

And also join in welcoming our guest from Israel, Brokim Abayim.

Preventing Iran from acquiring a nuclear weapon and curbing their malign regional and global influence is of paramount importance for American national security and the security of our allies. We must be clear-eyed in what actions move us closer and those that move us further away from this objective.

While I oppose the JCPOA, now that it is in place, we must aggressively and rigorously enforce it. The urgent responsibility of our Government at this time, in conjunction with our partners and our regional allies, is to develop that comprehensive strategy that will commit the necessary resources to work to close the gaps and reduce the risk of the JCPOA, including those sunset provisions.

I believe that President Trump's decision not to certify under the terms of INARA jeopardizes the restrictions already in place on Iran's nuclear activity at a time when we should be urgently working to shore up the Iran deal's shortcomings and holding Iran to account for its dangerous behavior outside the agreement. That includes Iran's support for Hezbollah and other terrorist proxies, illicit weapons transfers, ballistic missile program, and its human rights abuses. The President's decision risks isolating us from our international allies at the exact moment we need to work together to accomplish these goals.

I look forward to hearing from our witnesses today on how best to move forward to put an end to Iran's destabilizing behavior in the region and around the world, and ensure Iran is never able— never able—to acquire a nuclear weapon.

I yield back.

Ms. Ros-Lehtinen. Thank you very much, Mr. Schneider.

And seeing no further requests for time, I will introduce our witness.

But I would like to remind the audience members that disruption of committee proceedings is against the law and will not be tolerated. Although wearing themed shirts while seated in the hearing room is permissible, holding up signs during the proceedings is not. Any disruptions will result in a suspension of the proceedings until the Capitol Police can restore order.

And I am so pleased to welcome our witnesses here this morning. I would like to welcome back a good friend of our committee, Dr. Olli Heinonen, who is the Senior Advisor on Science and Nonproliferation at the Foundation for Defense of Democracies. Prior to this, Mr. Heinonen served as Deputy Director General of the International Atomic Energy Agency and as head of its Department of Safeguards. Dr. Heinonen is also a Senior Fellow at the Harvard Kennedy School of Government's Belfer Center for Science and International Affairs. We always look forward to your testimony, Dr. Heinonen. Thank you for being here.

And next, I am pleased to welcome back Ambassador Mark Wallace, who is the Chief Executive Officer of United Against Nuclear Iran, UANI, and the Counter-Extremism Project. Prior to funding UANI, he served as Ambassador to the United Nations, Representative for U.N. Management and Reform. Thank you for your service, Ambassador, and we look forward to your testimony.

And finally, we would like to welcome Dr. Philip Gordon. He is the Mary and David Boies Senior Fellow in U.S. Foreign Policy at the Council on Foreign Relations and a Senior Advisor at Albright Stonebridge Group. Dr. Gordon served on the National Security Council as a Special Assistant to the President and as the White House Coordinator for the Middle East, North Africa, and the Gulf Region. Dr. Gordon also served as Assistant Secretary of State for Europe and Eurasian Affairs. Thank you so much, Dr. Gordon, and we look forward to your testimony.

And as I said, your testimony will be made a part of the record. We will begin with Dr. Heinonen. Thank you.

STATEMENT OF OLLI HEINONEN, PH.D., SENIOR ADVISOR ON SCIENCE AND NONPROLIFERATION, FOUNDATION FOR DEFENSE OF DEMOCRACIES (FORMER DEPUTY DIRECTOR GENERAL OF THE INTERNATIONAL ATOMIC ENERGY AGENCY)

Mr. HEINONEN. Chairman Ros-Lehtinen and Ranking Member Deutch, thank you for giving me the opportunity to speak today about the President's decision, the next steps.

I will focus on the verification aspects of the JCPOA. Its advocates have characterized it as being the most intrusive nuclear inspection regime ever. They also claim that the measures put in place by the JCPOA block all of Iran's pathways to a nuclear weapon.

To the point of JCPOA verifications, I would like to argue that more forceful implementation and enforcement is needed. As for the deal's ability to block Iran's nuclear weapons pathway, it is not that simple. Indeed, arms control and nonproliferation agreements do not guarantee that the state will be blocked from getting nuclear weapons. They seek to deter it via early detection. Such deterrence is only successful when comprehensive verification measures are fully implemented in a manner that covers both declared and undeclared nuclear activities and facilities in a state. And as some of the terms of the JCPOA begin to sunset as early as 6 years from now, Iran's nuclear program will be in a stronger position capability-wise with a lower breakout time.

To address a number of the JCPOA's flaws, the deal's implementation provisions must be made far more robust and meaningful. To that end, several additional measures are necessary, and I would like to make to this end six points.

First, the IAEA's quarterly reports on the deal's implementation must be enhanced by providing more details on the actual implementation of the deal by the IAEA and on Iran's adherence to its obligations. Such requests are consistent with Article 5 of the IAEA Iran Safeguards Agreement, which authorizes the IAEA Board of Governors to be provided with the information necessary for the implementation of the agreement. My written testimony lists a number of specific suggestions which would make the reports on Iran more transparent, enabling readers to assess independently and in a timely manner progress made and any obstacles encountered.

Second, the IAEA should complete the followup access related to its investigation of the possible military dimensions of the Iranian nuclear program. These include site visits, interviews with the scientists, and investigating the reason for the presence of uranium particles at Parchin. It is also essential to establish a baseline for future verification that nuclear-weapons-related activities have not, and will not, be reconstituted in Iran. The IAEA has to be more specific in reporting its verification activities related to JCPOA's Section T, which prohibits activities which could contribute to the design and development of a nuclear explosive device.

Third, the JCPOA and related agreements must apply to all sides related to the Iranian nuclear program, with no exceptions to military sites or any other sites. For instance, given the fact that Iran manufactured most of its key components, such as centrifuge rotors and bellows, at military-owned workshops, those sites with the necessary expertise and tools should be subject to the monitoring.

Fourth, Iran should ratify the Additional Protocol well before the sunset provisions take effect and before the IAEA issues a broader conclusion about the nature of Iran's nuclear program. In accordance with the IAEA verification principles, a broader conclusion is only drawn when the Additional Protocol is ratified and fully implemented. There is no reason why Iran should be an exception from such a practice.

Fifth, Security Council Resolution 2231, limitations on ballistic missiles, should be extended to cruise missiles, while the restrictions on missile ranges and payloads should be lowered.

Sixth, and the last, but not the least, Iran's 1-year breakout time should be extended indefinitely into the future, while enabling more effective enforcement. By maintaining a breakout time of at least 1 year, it would ensure that the U.S. will have sufficient time to respond to Iran's violations before it crosses the nuclear weapons threshold. Current breakout time is calculated based both on the number and type of centrifuges Iran has installed as well as known amounts of uranium feed materials available. This is not enough. What needs to be also included in the estimates is the size and types of stocks of uninstalled centrifuges as well as the time required for their commissioning. They also need to take into account Iran's nuclear capabilities as it continues its R&D on better centrifuges.

And as the IAEA is far from determining that there are no undetected nuclear material and activities in Iran, it makes sense to build in uncertainties and create a buffer into our calculations. In other words, current calculated breakout time needs to be continually evaluated and new caps should be set as appropriate.

Thank you.

[The prepared statement of Mr. Heinonen follows:]

House Foreign Affairs Committee
Subcommittee on the Middle East and North Africa

The President's Iran Decision:

Next Steps

OLLI HEINONEN, PH.D.

Senior Advisor on Science and Nonproliferation
Foundation for Defense of Democracies

**Former Deputy Director General and
Head of Department of Safeguards**
International Atomic Energy Agency

Washington, DC
October 25, 2017

www.defenddemocracy.org

Olli Heinonen   October 25, 2017

The preamble to the Joint Comprehensive Plan of Action (JCPOA) asserts that the "full implementation" of the deal "will ensure the exclusively peaceful nature of Iran's nuclear program." In addition, the full implementation of the JCPOA "will positively contribute to regional and international peace and security."[1] More than two years have now passed since the conclusion of the JCPOA. Therefore, it is a good time to review those aspects of the deal that require strengthening if the JCPOA hopes to deny Iran access to a nuclear weapons capability.

UN Security Council Resolution 2231 endorsed the JCPOA's restrictions on Iran's uranium enrichment and plutonium recovery, while adding restraints on Iran's ballistic missile activities. These restrictions will be lifted when the JCPOA sunset clauses kick in. Six years from now, Iran will be able to start manufacturing advanced centrifuges, enabling it to gradually cut down its one-year nuclear breakout time. At the same time, if not earlier, restrictions on Iran's missile program will be terminated.

The time to act is now, and not six years from now when the sunset clauses begin to take effect. It will be far harder to fix the deal once sunset clauses help Iran to permanently establish itself as a threshold nuclear state with the capability to manufacture and deliver nuclear warheads in a short period of time. Iran's Foreign Minister Javad Zarif himself has stated that Iran will emerge from the deal with a stronger nuclear program.[2]

To increase the likelihood that the JCPOA ensures the peaceful nature of the Iranian nuclear program, there must be a far more robust and meaningful verification of the deal's provisions. To that end, several measures will be necessary. First, the IAEA's quarterly reports on the deal's implementation must be enhanced, preferably in the manner I describe below. Next, the IAEA should complete the follow-up actions related to its investigation of the Possible Military Dimensions (PMD) of the Iranian nuclear program, including site visits and interviews with scientists.[3] Third, the JCPOA and related agreements must apply to all sites related to the Iranian nuclear program, with no exceptions for military sites or any others. Fourth, Iran should ratify the Additional Protocol well before the sunset provisions take effect and before the IAEA issues a Broader Conclusion about the peaceful nature of the Iranian nuclear program. Fifth, the UNSCR 2231 limitations on ballistic missiles should be extended to cruise missiles, while the restrictions on missile ranges and payloads should be lowered. Finally, these and other measures should extend Iran's one-year breakout time indefinitely into the future, while enabling more effective enforcement.

---

[1] Joint Comprehensive Plan of Action, Vienna, July 14, 2015, Preamble Section ii and Preface first paragraph. (https://medium.com/@ObamaWhiteHouse/joint-comprehensive-plan-of-action-5cdd9b320fd)

[2] Julian Borger, "Iran's foreign minister urges Europe to defy US if Trump sinks nuclear deal," *The Guardian* (UK), September 29, 2017. (https://www.theguardian.com/world/2017/sep/29/iran-foreign-minister-zarif-europe-trump-nuclear)

[3] From 2002 onwards, the IAEA became increasingly concerned about the possible existence of undisclosed, nuclear-related activities in Iran involving military-related organizations, including activities related to the development of a nuclear payload for a missile. Subsequently, the IAEA identified outstanding issues related to these possible military dimensions of Iran's nuclear program, as well as actions required by Iran to resolve these issues. The IAEA issued its PMD findings in the report: International Atomic Energy Agency, "Final Assessment on Past and Present Outstanding Issues Regarding Iran's Nuclear Programme," December 2, 2015. (https://www.iaea.org/sites/default/files/gov-2015-68.pdf)

Olli Heinonen

The JCPOA – Does it block all of Iran's pathways to a nuclear weapon?

Advocates of the JCPOA have repeatedly asserted that Iran is now subject to the most intrusive nuclear inspection regime ever. Furthermore, the measures put in place by the JCPOA promised to "block all of Iran's pathways to a nuclear weapon."[4] It is not quite that simple. Arms control and nonproliferation agreements do not guarantee that a state will be blocked from getting nuclear weapons. A better metric against which to measure the JCPOA's effectiveness is the goal of deterrence via early detection. Such deterrence is only possible when verification measures are fully and meaningfully implemented in a manner that applies to both declared and undeclared nuclear activities and facilities.

Iran's nuclear weapons capability can be thought of as a tent with two main poles: the ability to build a nuclear warhead and the ability to deliver it. In most cases, this delivery is accomplished by missiles. To restrict the latter, UNSCR 2231 includes an ambiguous provision that "calls" on Iran not to develop and test missiles designed to be capable of carrying nuclear weapons.[5] To prevent the former, the IAEA is charged with implementing a verification system based on three related agreements: Iran's comprehensive safeguards agreement,[6] the Additional Protocol,[7] and the JCPOA – although some of the JCPOA's measures will start to fade away in just six years.[8]

Additional constraints needed for Iran's missile program

Iran's ballistic and cruise missiles tests have demonstrated a reach of thousands of kilometers.[9] The growing range of Iranian missiles indicates Tehran's desire to go beyond pure deterrence.[10] Experts at the UN Security Council have acknowledged that some of these missiles are capable of carrying nuclear warheads.[11] Despite such cause for concern, the ballistic missile limitations set

---

[4] The White House, "The Historic Deal that Will Prevent Iran from Acquiring a Nuclear Weapon: How the U.S. and the international community will block all of Iran's pathways to a nuclear weapon," accessed October 23, 2017. (https://obamawhitehouse.archives.gov/node/328996)

[5] United Nations Security Council, Resolution 2231, July 20, 2015. (https://www.iaea.org/sites/default/files/unsc_resolution2231-2015.pdf)

[6] State parties to the Nuclear Nonproliferation Treaty (NPT) have to conclude a Comprehensive Safeguards Agreement (CSA) with the IAEA. Under a CSA. the IAEA has the right and obligation to ensure that safeguards are applied on all nuclear material in the territory, jurisdiction, or control of the state for the exclusive purpose of verifying that such material is not diverted to nuclear weapons or other nuclear explosive devices.

[7] The Additional Protocol (AP) is a legal document granting the IAEA complementary inspection authority to that provided in underlying safeguards agreements. A principal aim of the AP is to enable the IAEA to provide better assurances about both declared and possible undeclared activities. Under the AP, the IAEA is granted expanded rights of access to information and sites.

[8] Examples on such measures are monitoring of uranium mines, production of uranium ore concentrate, production of heavy water. manufacturing of centrifuge rotors and bellows, and installation of advanced centrifuges.

[9] "Iranian Missile Launches: 1988-Present," *Center for Strategic and International Studies*, October 12, 2017. (https://missilethreat.csis.org/iranian-missile-launches-1988-present/)

[10] David Cooper. "Nebulous Language Enables Tehran's Missile Ambitions." *The Cipher Brief*, September 1, 2017. (https://www.thecipherbrief.com/article/middle-east/nebulous-language-enables-tehrans-missile-ambitions?utm_source=Join+the+Community+Subscribers&utm_campaign=82ca1db268-TCB+Sept+1+2017&utm_medium=email&utm_term=0_02cbee778d-82ea1db268-122476009)

[11] United Nations Security Council, 7990th meeting, June 29, 2017. (http://www.securitycouncilreport.org/atf/cf/%7B65BFCF9B-6D27-4E9C-8CD3-CF6E4FF96FF9%7D/s_pv_7990.pdf)

Olli Heinonen   October 25, 2017

by UNSC Resolution 2231 expire six years from now, at most.[12] This expiration would give Iran free rein to develop its missile capabilities about the time the JCPOA permits Iran to start expanding its uranium enrichment capabilities, which could generate fissile material for nuclear warheads. Thus, any effort to fix the JCPOA or negotiate a complementary agreement should provide for capping the range of Iranian missiles and extending restrictions to cruise missiles currently under development.[13]

Additionally, due to the weakened language of Resolution 2231, there is no systematic monitoring of Iran's missile procurement efforts by the Security Council. This is a serious problem as indicated by reports from German intelligence agencies, which exposed about 30 such attempts in 2016, even after the implementation of the nuclear deal.[14] The most direct means to address this problem is to amend Resolution 2231. If Russia or China is determined to block such a revision, the U.S. should use bilateral contacts with partners to press for the exposure of Iran's illicit acquisition of missile technologies. The U.S. should also consider whether it would be possible to rectify the situation by imposing secondary sanctions on foreign companies and banks that facilitate illicit Iranian procurement efforts.

Iran's commitments to remain a non-nuclear weapons state

Under the JCPOA, Iran commits itself not to acquire and develop nuclear weapons. Tehran has made such commitments before, yet the IAEA then uncovered a clandestine nuclear program with possible military dimensions.

Foreign Minister Javad Zarif has warned that if the U.S. withdraws from the nuclear deal, "then we're not bound by that agreement and we will then decide how we want to deal with it." "It does not mean that Iran wants to pursue a nuclear weapons option," Zarif said, "But what is important is if the deal is broken, then Iran has many options, one of which would be to have an unlimited yet peaceful nuclear energy program."[15]

As a party to the Nuclear Nonproliferation Treaty (NPT),[16] Iran has frequently affirmed it has no desire for nuclear weapons. But in 2003, the IAEA found Iran in breach of its nuclear obligations

---

[12] The IAEA draws a "broader conclusion" only in countries with both a comprehensive safeguards agreement and an additional protocol in force, and when the IAEA has sufficient information and access to provide credible assurances to the international community of both the non-diversion of declared nuclear material from peaceful nuclear activities and the absence of undeclared nuclear material and activities. International Atomic Energy Agency, "Nuclear Safeguards Conclusions Presented in 2016 Safeguards Implementation Report," June 16, 2017. (https://www.iaea.org/newscenter/news/nuclear-safeguards-conclusions-presented-in-2016-safeguards-implementation-report)

[13] Olli Heinonen, "Iran's missile tests reveal weaknesses of UN Security Council Resolution," *Foundation for Defense of Democracies,* February 8, 2017. (http://www.defenddemocracy.org/media-hit/olli-heinonen1-irans-missile-tests-reveal-weaknesses-of-un-security-council-resolution/)

[14] Benjamin Weinthal, "Iran accused of trying to develop nuclear-tipped missiles," *Fox News.* October 20. 2017. (http://www.defenddemocracy.org/media-hit/benjamin-weinthal-iran-accused-of-trying-to-develop-nuclear-tipped-missiles/)

[15] "Zarif: Nuclear renegotiation is a 'myth,'" *Tehran Times* (Iran), October 1, 2017. (http://www.tehrantimes.com/news/417199/Zarif-Nuclear-renegotiation-is-a-myth)

[16] The NPT aims to prevent the spread of nuclear weapons and weapons technology, to foster the peaceful uses of nuclear energy, and to further the goal of disarmament. The treaty establishes a safeguards system under the

Olli Heinonen   October 25, 2017

under the comprehensive safeguards agreement meant to ensure its fidelity to the NPT. Further IAEA investigations revealed that Iran had conducted a range of activities related to the development of a nuclear explosive device, which continued to some extent at least until 2009.[17] Only the rigorous enforcement of a strict verification regime can help deter Iran from pursuing nuclear weapons.

Iran needs to ratify the Additional Protocol (AP)

Additional Protocols (APs) are complementary arrangements intended to strengthen the comprehensive safeguards agreements adopted by parties to the NPT. In 2003, following the initial revelations that it had violated its safeguards agreement, Iran signed its AP and agreed to implement the agreement provisionally, but ceased the implementation in 2005. Under the JCPOA, Iran has likewise agreed to implement the AP provisionally, while pledging to ratify the AP once the IAEA reaches a "broader conclusion" that the Iranian nuclear program is entirely peaceful. However, there is no fixed dead line for ratification. This is not an insignificant matter and should be addressed for two reasons. First, in accordance with IAEA verification principles, a "broader conclusion" has only been drawn (to date) when an AP is ratified and fully implemented. There are no reasons why Iran should be an exception from such a practice. Second, Iran has been slow in fulfilling its other nuclear promises. Tehran stated in 2003 that it would sign and ratify the IAEA's Nuclear Safety Convention (NSC), but has not done so to date. This effectively makes Iran the only country – apart from North Korea – that has industrial-scale nuclear facilities not covered the NSC. Advocates of the JCPOA who point to the AP containing many commitments that will never sunset are pointing to a provisional implementation until the AP is actually ratified.

Enforcing and updating a one-year breakout time

One of the key goals of the JCPOA is to ensure that Iran will remain at least one year away from developing enough fissile material for a nuclear warhead. This one-year interval is known as Iran's "breakout time." The length of this breakout time depends on both the number and sophistication of the centrifuges Iran has installed, as well as the size of its stockpile of enriched uranium and centrifuges yet to be installed. In theory, maintaining a breakout time of at least one year would ensure that the U.S. and its partners have sufficient time to respond to Iran violations before its crosses the nuclear weapons threshold.

Iran committed, as part of the JCPOA, to decrease its stock of about 19,000 installed centrifuges to just 6,104, with only 5,060 of these designated for enriching uranium. This restriction will last for ten years, and all of the centrifuges will be first-generation models known as IR-1s. However, the nuclear deal does allow Iran to engage in limited research and development with its advanced centrifuges, including the IR-2m, IR-4, IR-5, IR-6, IR-7, and IR-8 models. In addition, the JCPOA caps the size of Iran's stockpile at 300 kilograms of 3.67-percent enriched uranium for the next

---

responsibility of the IAEA, which also plays a central role under in the area of technology transfer for peaceful purposes. Under Article II of the treaty, the state undertakes not to receive nuclear weapons or other nuclear explosive devices and not to manufacture or otherwise acquire them, as well as not to seek or receive any assistance in the manufacture of nuclear weapons or other nuclear explosive devices.

[17] International Atomic Energy Agency, "Final Assessment on Past and Present Outstanding Issues regarding Iran's Nuclear Programme," December 2, 2015. (https://www.iaea.org/sites/default/files/gov-2015-68.pdf)

Olli Heinonen										October 25, 2017

fifteen years (e.g. uranium that contains 3.67 percent of the fissile isotope U-235).

Calculating breakout time depends on the number and types of centrifuges Iran has installed or could install from its current stock, as well as inventories of uranium feed materials. The estimated one-year breakout time reflects calculations based on the physical caps that the JCPOA imposes on Iran's centrifuge stocks as well as the natural and enriched uranium feed material available. What such calculations do not take into account is the potential for Iran to learn from experience how to enrich more efficiently, or to employ dual-use equipment allowed by the JCPOA. In addition, when the sunset clauses come into effect, this will further reduce Iran's breakout. Taking all these factors into consideration, current breakout time markers need to be periodically reviewed and constraints revisited.[18] It also makes good sense to build in uncertainties and create a buffer when calculating a one-year breakout time, rather than relying on calculations that apply to best-case scenarios.

Efforts to calculate Tehran's breakout time should also not discount possible undeclared nuclear activities in Iran. While it is fairly easy to verify and monitor declared enrichment locations and nuclear materials, it is much more difficult to provide good assurances regarding the absence of undeclared nuclear materials and centrifuges Iran could have manufactured but not reported to the IAEA. In a report from June 2004, the IAEA noted that activities such as centrifuge component production in Iran are inherently difficult to verify without extensive inspections and historical knowledge. As such, the assurances that the Agency can provide are of a different nature from those achievable with respect to the diversion of nuclear material from declared sites.[19]

What does this mean in terms of enforcing a one-year breakout? Given the fact that Iran manufactured most of its key components such as centrifuge rotors and bellows at military-owned workshops, those sites should be subject to monitoring. At those workshops, Iran very likely retains the necessary machine tools for centrifuge manufacturing, while military personnel likely still have the expertise necessary to manufacture those pieces.

Discovering a clandestine enrichment or manufacturing installation is a difficult task, as shown by the revelation of the Fordow enrichment plant in September 2009. When exposed, Fordow was at an advanced stage of installation. Applying the lessons of Fordow means that the parties to the nuclear deal must close off the loopholes and interpretations that place the JCPOA in a weaker rather than stronger position. For example, Iran should be subject to "anytime, anywhere" inspections, understood per standard inspection procedures as 24-hour complementary access, including to military sites, in contrast to the JCPOA's 24-day timeframe. JCPOA negotiators have stated that the 24-day timeframe in no way prevents more rapid access, since 24 days is the maximum time allowed when accessing undeclared locations. On this point it is worth remembering that the 24-hour delay permitted by the Additional Protocol was to allow for administrative hold-ups while preserving the element of a surprise visit. There is no justification for a longer waiting period and the default should continue to remain at 24 hours.

---

[18] Olli Heinonen and Simon Henderson, "How to Make Sure Iran's One-Year Nuclear Breakout Time Does Not Shrink," *The Washington Institute for Near East Policy*, June 17, 2015. (http://www.washingtoninstitute.org/policy-analysis/view/how-to-make-sure-irans-one-year-nuclear-breakout-time-does-not-shrink)

[19] International Atomic Energy Agency, "Implementation of the NPT Safeguards Agreement in the Islamic Republic of Iran," June 1, 2004. (https://www.iaea.org/sites/default/files/gov2004-34.pdf)

                                                                    October 25, 2017

To preserve a one-year breakout period, it is also indispensable for the IAEA to report quarterly –
and in a transparent manner – on Iran's holdings and production of enrichment feed material,
uranium hexafluoride (UF6), stocks of all types of centrifuges and rotors, and installations
involved in manufacturing of the key components of centrifuges. Several member states have
already requested such reporting at IAEA meetings. The secretariat should follow up on these
requests expeditiously. Such requests are consistent with Article 5 of IAEA safeguards
agreements, which forbids the dissemination of confidential proprietary information but
specifically allows information relating to the implementation of agreements to be given to the
Board of Governors.[20] Moreover, there is ample precedent for this kind of information sharing.
Prior IAEA reports submitted as part of the EU-3 agreement with Iran presented both sufficient
details as well as the context necessary to understand the inspection findings. The United States
would be well within its right to introduce a resolution at the IAEA Board asking the secretariat to
make such information available to the Board.

The case for IAEA access to military sites in Iran

Iranian leaders have declared that they will never allow IAEA inspectors to access military sites.
This position is completely at odds with both the JCPOA and Iran's comprehensive safeguards
agreement.

Iran's military industry has played a well-documented and important role in developing the
country's domestic manufacturing capacities. In 2003, half a dozen military-related workshops
provided their services to the Atomic Energy Organization's efforts at uranium enrichment.
Additionally, the Fordow underground enrichment plant was built on a military site.

Under Article 1 of the IAEA comprehensive safeguards agreement, all nuclear facilities and
materials inside state territory are subject to IAEA safeguards.[21] Thus, there are no sanctuaries
from which inspectors can be excluded – including military sites.

In the case of Iran, inspectors should request access to:
- Confirm that Iran is not conducting centrifuge manufacturing activities at locations where
  it was doing such work before the JCPOA;
- Address issues from the PMD file that remain unresolved, including interviews of scientists
  and follow-up regarding the uranium particles found at Parchin;[22]
- Establish a baseline for future verification that nuclear weapons-related activities have not
  been reconstituted; and

---

[20] International Atomic Energy Agency, "The Text of the Agreement Between Iran and The International Atomic
Energy Agency for the Application of Safeguards in Connection with the Treaty on the Non-Proliferation of Nuclear
Weapons," December 13, 1974.
(https://www.iaea.org/sites/default/files/publications/documents/infcircs/1974/infcirc214.pdf)
[21] Ibid.
[22] Olli Heinonen, "Uranium Particles at Parchin Indicate Possible Undeclared Iranian Nuclear Activities."
Foundation for Defense of Democracies, July 1, 2016. (http://www.defenddemocracy.org/media-hit/olli-heinonen1-
uranium-particles-at-parchin-indicate-possible-undeclared-iranian-nuclear-a/)

- Verify and monitor the JCPOA's Section T, which prohibits "activities which could contribute to the design and development of a nuclear explosive device."[23]

Since January 2016, when the JCPOA was implemented, IAEA reports have made no mention of verifying the first three items listed above. In June 2017, the IAEA's quarterly report stated, "The Agency's verification and monitoring of Iran's other JCPOA nuclear-related commitments continues, including those set out in Sections D, E, S and T of Annex I of the JCPOA." The report, however, provides no details on whether the IAEA actually verified Section T via first-hand observation or simply reviewed publications indicating relevant activities in the open literature. Even more significant, an IAEA staff member in a background briefing made a statement to the effect that the IAEA had not visited any military site since the JCPOA's implementation.[24] It is difficult to comprehend why a follow-up visit has not taken place at Parchin, where uranium particles were found in 2015. The IAEA has also presented evidence that Parchin hosted research related to multi-point detonations and the use of diagnostic equipment as part of a nuclear weapons research program.

It is crucial that the U.S. and its allies encourage the IAEA to faithfully conduct its mission and not shy away from seeking entry to sensitive sites in Iran where there is cause to do so. Continued investigation of the history of the possible military dimension of Iran's nuclear program must also continue. Indeed, the Additional Protocol specifically seeks to ensure, via additional access rights for the IAEA, that there is no indication of undeclared nuclear materials or activities in a state. Given the clandestine, complex, and possible military aspects of Iran's nuclear work, no military sites should be accepted as off limits. One option for the United States to consider is the introduction of a resolution at an IAEA Board meeting requesting that the secretariat complete verification activities related to the PMD file and Section T of the JCPOA.

IAEA reporting has to be enhanced

The IAEA has critical a role to play in preventing nuclear proliferation, thanks to its inspectorate's unique authority to access people, places, and facilities. The IAEA's full exercise of these rights is indispensable to the full and meaningful implementation of the JCPOA. It is equally necessary for IAEA investigations to produce impartial, factual, and transparent reports of its findings in written form. The importance of written reporting must be underscored since it represents the official record of its findings; any statements made by the IAEA secretariat in technical briefings -- albeit helpful -- are not entered in the official records.

It is also important to understand how to read the IAEA reports. For example, the secretariat states that it continues to verify the non-diversion of declared nuclear material in Iran, but it has not explicitly stated that there are no indications of diversion of nuclear material from declared inventories. The IAEA report states that Iran is implementing certain parts of the JCPOA. For other

---

[23] Such activities include computer models to simulate nuclear explosive devices, multi-point detonation, and diagnostic systems suitable for the development of nuclear explosive devices and explosively driven neutron sources.

[24] Francois Murphy. "U.S. pressure or not, U.N. nuclear watchdog sees no need to check Iran military sites," *Reuters*, August 31, 2017. (http://www.reuters.com/article/us-iran-nuclear-inspections/u-s-pressure-or-not-u-n-nuclear-watchdog-sees-no-need-to-check-iran-military-sites-idUSKCN1BB1JC)

Olli Heinonen

parts of the JCPOA, such as the implementation of Section T, the IAEA has simply not reported on it or, as in its most recent report, simply states that it is monitoring it, but fails to explain how and to what extent such monitoring is conducted. Even in terms of implementation, the IAEA reports do not provide a clear picture of how and to what extent compliance with the JCPOA is understood. In other words, to ensure proper implementation, IAEA reports should provide more clarity by stating whether Iran has fully complied with its obligations, whether the IAEA has had full and timely access to all installations subject to verification and monitoring, and whether it has received all the information it requested. The IAEA should also provide greater clarity with regard to how verification and monitoring measures are being applied.

To be able to ensure that break-out time remains above one year, and to assess the implementation of the JCPOA and the safeguards agreements, the United States should request – as is permitted by Article 5 of the safeguards agreement – that the following additional facts be included to future quarterly reports:

- Uranium mining and ore concentration plants: IAEA reports should include, for example, the number of visits to mines and ore concentration plants, if access was provided in a timely fashion, and the amounts of ore concentrates (yellow cake) produced.

- Uranium conversion (to UF6 and UO_2) activities: IAEA reports should include information on the stocks of uranium ore concentrates, stocks of UF6 (feed material for uranium enrichment), stocks of UO_2, and the operating status of the conversion facilities.

- Uranium enrichment activities: IAEA reports should include information on the type and amount of uranium fed into cascades at each facility, the type and number of centrifuges installed at the Natanz Fuel Enrichment and Pilot Fuel Enrichment Plants, the number and types of centrifuge rotors stored under IAEA surveillance at Natanz, an assessment on whether IAEA surveillance measures are conclusive, and if complementary access and unannounced inspection access was provided in a timely fashion.

Conclusion

More than two years have now passed since the conclusion of the JCPOA. This is a good time to review areas of the deal that require strengthening in order to deny Iran access to a nuclear weapons capability, keep Iran well within the desired one-year breakout time, and to reevaluate the sunset clauses. It is important that both Iran and the IAEA fully implement their obligations under the JCPOA, CSA, and AP. Likewise, the IAEA should enhance its reporting on Iran's compliance with its obligations, and the IAEA Board has the authority to require more detailed reports.

The parties to the JCPOA should agree on parameters that keep Iran's nuclear breakout time above one year in perpetuity. In exchange for this restriction, the U.S. and its partners should consider providing Iran with nuclear fuel assurances and spent fuel take-back guarantees to deny it a rationale for further enrichment and reprocessing. Another key part of the conversation is to refocus attention on Iran's offensive ballistic and cruise missile program, with the goal of bringing it down to shorter ranges and payloads. Iran has repeatedly stated that the JCPOA is not

Olli Heinonen   October 25, 2017

negotiable,[25] but there might be ways and means to complement the deal with additional binding arrangements.

---

[25] "Zarif: Nuclear renegotiation is a 'myth,'" *Tehran Times* (Iran), October 1, 2017. (http://www.tehrantimes.com/news/417199/Zarif-Nuclear-renegotiation-is-a-myth)

Ms. Ros-Lehtinen. Thank you very much. Good recommendations, well-thought-out.

Ambassador Wallace, pleased to hear from you.

STATEMENT OF THE HONORABLE MARK WALLACE , CHIEF EXECUTIVE OFFICER, UNITED AGAINST NUCLEAR IRAN (FORMER U.S. AMBASSADOR TO THE UNITED NATIONS FOR MANAGEMENT AND REFORM)

Ambassador Wallace. Thank you, Madam Chairman and Ranking Member Deutch. It is an honor to be on this panel with my two colleagues, and I would also like to acknowledge my many United Against Nuclear Iran colleagues that are behind me.

At the outset, I must express my appreciation to you, Madam Chairman, for your service to this nation.

Ms. Ros-Lehtinen. The gentleman is recognized for as much time as needed. [Laughter.]

Ambassador Wallace. I was going to ask the ranking member for the same indulgence, and I expected the same courtesy.

I have appeared several times and worked with this committee for many years, and this is perhaps my last time in front of you, as you will be stepping down after a distinguished career. It is too soon to roll out the roasting and all of that business.

Ms. Ros-Lehtinen. It is never too soon.

Ambassador Wallace. All right. But, since I am originally from Miami, Florida, and we both have a passion about University of Miami football and we have worked a little bit on Iran over the years, I think it is important that I speak about you for just a little bit of my time—just a little bit.

You have been a trailblazer as the first Hispanic woman elected to Congress and the first female chairman of the House Foreign Affairs Committee. But, going beyond symbolism, the secrets to your success in Washington are simple. Your kindness, your courage, your decency, and in my opinion most importantly—and Congressman Deutch was speaking to this—your moral compass, are all far rare attributes that need to be here in Washington. I am not going to talk about the time you accidentally hung up on President Obama after your reelection.

You have never been afraid to take the lead on difficult issues. You have bucked your own party on countless occasions, notably being the first Republican to support a bill repealing the Defense of Marriage Act. And in foreign policy you have become a dictator's worst nightmare. Fidel Castro once dubbed you "the big bad wolf," a term you have worn as a badge of honor. But I am particularly thankful for your leadership on Iran policy.

My friend, we will miss you. I have a feeling that, even when you do step down, you won't be quiet or silent, but I don't think I am going to be here or have an opportunity again before you go, but we will miss you. And I know I speak for everyone in the room on that.

Now, to more serious business, Henry Kissinger famously said that the Islamic Republic of Iran must decide whether it is a nation or a cause. Nonetheless, those who focus on the role Iran has chosen to play in the world will rightly acknowledge that its leadership has definitely proven to be both a nation as well as a cause.

While discussion of the JCPOA may be the first priority for Congress, we must put this into context. Regardless of one's view on the deal's utility, one cannot gainsay the fact that the geostrategic posture of Iran has improved dramatically since its ratification. For both the United States as well as Iran, the JCPOA may prove to be a sideshow. Yes, it is terribly flawed and should be fixed, if possible. Nonetheless, the overarching issue facing both the administration and Congress is meeting the challenge that Iranian hegemony now poses in the region.

The administration has proposed a policy of rollback. It is Congress' duty to go even beyond this and to both hold the administration's feet to the fire and provide the mechanisms for this policy to be implemented. Only through this strategic reassessment and a robust collaboration between our executive and legislative branches can America's honor be restored and its interests truly be served.

President Rouhani's own words on Monday show why this is so important. He said, "The greatness of the nation of Iran and the region is more than at any other time. . . . In Iraq, Syria, Lebanon, North Africa, and the Persian Gulf region, where can action be taken without Iran?" That is what President Rouhani said.

We propose a variety of steps in my more detailed testimony. And one of the things I was going to emphasize here was perhaps suggesting we begin with FTO designation of the Quds Force as a solution.

We provide a lot of different recommendations, but I am throwing away the notes for a minute because this is your last time and may be my last time in front of you. But I want to go to what Mr. Deutch said and what you, Madam Chairman, said. Our relative advantage, what we have done is we have spent more time talking to business leaders and persons swirling around in the Iran space than anyone else. That is what we know.

And I will tell you what was the bipartisan consensus before that you guys led in a bipartisan manner. It was the notion that there would be ever-increasing pressure on Iran in a systematic way because of the work that you did and, then, the Treasury Department and the State Department and the White House would follow ever increasing that pressure. It worked. I am not a sanctions apologist. It doesn't work in all countries, but it worked in the context of Iran. Even my friends in the Obama administration lauded the effect of the sanctions regime in bringing Iran to the table. We have to get back to that place, and both of your comments reflect that.

I am happy to testify about a variety of those mechanisms. You all know them. They are different recipes to get to the same meal. But that is where we have to get because of their incredible expansionist activities in the region and the fact that I, too, believe the nuclear agreement was flawed.

Thank you.

[The prepared statement of Ambassador Wallace follows:]

AMBASSADOR MARK D. WALLACE
CEO, UNITED AGAINST NUCLEAR IRAN
TESTIMONY BEFORE THE U.S. HOUSE FOREIGN AFFAIRS COMMITTEE
SUBCOMMITTEE ON THE MIDDLE EAST AND NORTH AFRICA
OCTOBER 25, 2017

Chairman Ros-Lehtinen, Ranking Member Deutch, and members of the subcommittee, thank you for the opportunity to testify today, and thank you for your longstanding commitment and attention to these issues.

Unfortunately, the Iran nuclear deal—formally known as the Joint Comprehensive Plan of Action (JCPOA)—does not prevent a nuclear Iran. In fact, the JCPOA paves the way for Iran, in the not very long-term, to become a nuclear-armed state. For that reason, we opposed the agreement in 2015, and we support correcting its flaws now so that it ensures—in perpetuity—that Iran does not acquire or develop nuclear weapons.

Since Dr. Olli Heinonen is testifying, and he's as good a nonproliferation expert as it gets (and sits on UANI's Advisory Board), I'll defer to him on the technical problems with the JCPOA as it was constructed and as it's being implemented. Instead, I'll concentrate on what the United States government—and especially Congress—needs to do to achieve a better deal and a safer world.

The Regional Dynamic

Henry Kissinger famously said that the Islamic Republic of Iran must decide whether it is a nation or a cause. At the time, it was a brilliant observation. Nonetheless, those who focus on the role Iran has chosen to play in the world will rightly acknowledge that its leadership has deftly proven to be *both* a nation as well as a cause. Depending on the openings they are given to expand their reach, Tehran is equally comfortable, depending on the first principle of expediency, playing the role of guarantor of its Shia co-religionists or promoters of anti-Western militants, such as Palestinian extremists, if either posture will allow them to fill a vacuum. On occasion, the vacuum is created by their adversaries. In most instances, the vacuum is created by their own scheming. Either way, playing with the cards that are dealt or themselves deal, they are very, very good at "planting flags in Arab capitals," as they are wont to boast, and doing so with gusto.

While discussion of the JCPOA may be the first priority for Congress, we must put this into context. Regardless of one's view on the deal's utility, multiple regional experts routinely state that the geostrategic posture of Iran has improved dramatically since its ratification. Before the ink was dry, Iran embarked on its most aggressive imperial excursion in centuries, sending its own fighting men, as well as an expeditionary force of Shia fighters from other countries into Syria. With Russia, they changed the status quo from one of a countdown to the Assad regime's demise to a victory for one of the most cannibalistic governments in the world. Under cover of sanctions relief and its reinsertion into the global economy and polity, they made their move within months of the JCPOA's passage. It was a gamble that paid off. Iran and Russia, now for the first time in decades a power player in the region, call the shots, literally and figuratively. Along the way, they created through the suborning of chemical attacks and barrel bombs, the most politically impactful refugee crisis in the world today. As we have seen European politics upended by their handiwork—and America's own politics altered by the refugee crisis that has followed Assad's "win at all cost" strategy—the broader implications of Iran's initiatives, now under Russian air cover, cannot be overstated. The fact that Iran—itself a victim of chemical weapons during its war with Iraq—would stand by Assad after his repeated use of chemical weapons says much of Tehran's morality. With the exception perhaps of Russia, more than any other single country with whom we are adversaries, Iran is the one that is most actively working against our interests, and those of our closest allies, everywhere and all the time.

For both the United States as well as Iran, the JCPOA may prove to be a sideshow. Yes, it is terribly flawed and should be fixed. Yes, the sunset provisions have laid the groundwork for a nuclear arms race in the most destabilized part of the world today. And yes, through front-ended sanctions relief we have financed the very terror and Iranian expansionism that has characterized Iranian activities in the post-deal world. Nonetheless the overarching issue facing both the Administration and Congress is meeting the challenge that Iranian hegemony now poses in the region.

Congress's posture towards the decertification issue cannot but be colored by the way that the deal must remain in the American interest. There are those who say that trying to change the deal will lead to a weakening of America's word and the value of its promises. This is disingenuous. Nobody wants a world where its greatest power cannot be trusted. And yet, that is precisely the world in which we find ourselves. For in engineering the deal with Iran, and in ensuring its passage by Congress, the U.S. government broke so many red lines in its promises that the deal itself crushed America's credibility with most of its allies. Think back to when Iran was told it could not enrich, or that its nuclear program would need to be dismantled or face the risk of military attack. Allies who were resisting the Iranian position, particularly the French whose Foreign Minister famously rebelled against the momentum we created for a "sucker's deal," were overruled in favor of deep concessions that broke our word, not to mention the faith of all those who depended on America's word being sacred. The betrayal was brazen. The Gulf Arabs and Israelis, those most at risk of a nuclear-armed Iran and who have faced its subversion from Gaza to Bahrain and the Eastern Province of Saudi Arabia, were sidelined and told to accept whatever the United States put forward. "And for what?", one might ask. Everyone knows that, by the time the sunset provisions expire, the combination of sanctions relief and the inflow of Western, Chinese and Russian investment will have created such vested interests against military action that Iran will be allowed to break out. The Administration all but boasted at its ability to create what we now call "fake news" to give "snap back" credence. "Snap back," however, was a fraud. The coalition that nearly broke Iran's economy is now clamoring to gain access to Iran's market. Once invested, and already fatigued from the memory of the sanctions regime and long negotiations with the Iranians, the parties will never endorse military action under any guise. And so, in the absence of a realistic deterrent, the breakout will most likely occur with a whimper rather than a bang.

In sum, America's reputation for strength of purpose as well as a word that can be trusted is already in tatters. Some of us will remember how the term "containment" of Iran was viewed as suggestive of a less than robust posture and how Chuck Hagel, at his confirmation hearing to be secretary of defense, was rebuked for even suggesting such a supine posture. Today, as Iranian-backed expeditionary forces bath in the Mediterranean with impunity, Americans might wish that even that weak and discredited policy had been implemented. To compound this perfidy by insisting that we keep to a bad deal that literally betrayed those allies that have been on the front lines of their twilight struggle with Iranian subversion—in order to keep faith with the regime that bears the biggest responsibility for undermining all of our national interests in the region—is not merely nonsensical. It is perverse in its thinking. When one considers the way in which Iran's allies have slaughtered hundreds of thousands of Syrians with barrel bombs and chemicals, and created new conflicts that have resulted in the horrible deaths of hundreds of thousands more Arab men, women, and children from Iraq to Yemen, where they have sought to place Hezbollah on the straits of the Bab el Mandeb and trained militants who destabilize Bahrain, the reasoning that we debase the value of the promises contained within a document that could never have passed Congress as a treaty is more than *perverse*. It is, in its bloodsoaked cynicism not to mention abdication of reason as well as responsibility, nothing less than *perverted*.

The JCPOA was a brilliant stroke for Iran. As fine an example of patient Iranian statecraft as this might be, however, the absorption in plain sight of Iraq is proving to be their Finest Hour. One might even guess that this shall prove the title of Qasem Suleimani's memoirs. Far more than any other aspect of their activities, the reconfiguration of Iraq—or more accurately the parts of the country that they desire—into a satellite status and ultimately direct control is at the top of Tehran's list of strategic ambitions. Dominating Mesopotamia has been an enduring part of Persian, and then Iranian, imperial pretensions for millennia. The opening created by the American invasion, the vacuum created by an unsatisfactory exit by American forces, the fall of Mosul, our failure to honor red lines against Syria's use of chemical weapons, and dramatic emergence of ISIS have all coalesced into the most dramatic reshaping of the Middle Eastern landscape in the last century. Had America a less motivated adversary in Tehran, this might not have been the case. The outcomes could have been far more benign. But that was not to be. The IRGC and the theocrats are united in their promotion of a policy that promotes Shia interests to advance their own nationalistic agenda. In Iraq, this took the form of a sophisticated strategy. From a top down standpoint, the Iranians and their proxies encouraged the sectarian discrimination emanating from the Maliki Government that pushed the Sunnis to towards those who might protect them from the majority Shia. From the bottom up, they may have even done more to fan the flames that led to the collapse of Mosul. At the very least, they have ruthlessly exploited the chaos that was created with the emergence of ISIS and crystallized with the fall of Mosul, to put boots on the ground. It does not take a conspiracy theorist to guess who have been the major beneficiaries of the global threat posed by ISIS. It was the emergence of ISIS that has given Iran an excuse to intervene in Iraq and then Syria and, very importantly, to position itself as an ally with Russia and the West in a common war against Sunni extremism.

The importance of this new mantle of respectability is critical to the exercise. Rather than being seen as a troublemaker for the cynical meddling in which it has been engaged, Iran's willingness to intervene militarily after the fall of Mosul was actually cited by the previous Administration as a *justification* for compromising important deal points within the JCPOA, on the basis that diplomacy was already yielding fruits on the ground in a convergence of our foreign policy with that of Iran's. In effect, ISIS has proven to be the cat's paw for an adventurist fantasy that would have made the Shahs blush…building a land bridge from Iran to the Mediterranean. By filling a power vacuum left by American retreat and Arab turmoil, Tehran exploited a truly terrible Sunni movement that appalled the West to lubricate the case for armed intervention in favor of other equally terrible pro-Iran regimes. As statecraft abetted by tradecraft, it has been a brilliant success.

Whether or not Iran has actually abetted the rise of ISIS itself is still an open question—for years the world has read press reports of al-Qaeda operatives moving through Iran. But the underpinnings of such a conjecture is not without precedent, and indeed bear some reflection on the nature of the adversary with whom we're engaging. Remarkably flexible, indeed downright ecumenical, in their thinking, if there is a shared objective to weaken its rivals, Tehran sees no problem providing support and sanctuary to extremist Sunni organizations with whom they are otherwise at odds philosophically. As shown by an acknowledged outreach from Iran's proxy Hezbollah to the Muslim Brotherhood in Egypt both before and after the overthrow of Hosni Mubarak, there are clearly no limits to their philosophy that the anti-U.S. enemy of my enemy is my friend. This includes other Muslim Brotherhood offshoots such as the Islamic Jihad and Hamas in Gaza, the leadership of which is now being feted in Tehran. Their glee in killing Israelis is only matched by the glee with which the Iranian regime mocks the Holocaust. It even encompasses our own sworn enemies, Al-Qaeda, a number of whose leaders were given sanctuary in Iran. And then there remains the direct and lethal nexus between Iran and the killers of Americans in Afghanistan, the Taliban. Despite their blood feud with the Taliban, if the end result is the deaths of their most hated enemies, the Americans—the Great Satans—there are no limits to their ideological pragmatism. And there may be no limits to the body bags containing murdered Americans that are the bitter fruits of this poisonous tree.

All of these activities against our interests and citizens, and those of our allies, which UANI warned so strenuously against over the years, have only been abetted by the cash and political cover provided by the nuclear deal. Alas, Iran needed the JCPOA more than we did. By the time Rouhani was elected President, the regime was on the ropes. The deprivations created by the official sanctions regime and, as they acknowledged, the hammering they were taking from hated governments and private organizations, including UANI, required peace with the global community in order for them to recover their economic and political equilibrium. Our government hoped for the best. Theirs hoped to get Qasem Suleimani to Moscow as quickly as possible. We famously extended our hand in peace. They famously could not move fast enough to prop up the war criminals of Damascus. Tehran's end game, however, was no accident. They had already increased Iran's military budget 145 percent over the course of President Rouhani's first term. Simply put, America failed, or chose not to see, that Iran was playing chess while we were playing checkers.

We are not viscerally opposed to a future for the Middle East with a robust and thriving Iran. To the contrary, our hopes are with the aspirations of the Iranian people whom we truly believe seek freedom from the rule of the Mullahs and their lethal backbone, the IRGC's military-industrial complex. Nonetheless, as America has found in all the struggles we have faced with a determined enemy, we must deal with the reality of the regime that exists in Iran, not the one that we hope they will have one day. The first order of business, therefore, is to build a coalition capable of rolling back Iran's gains. They cannot be allowed to consolidate their land bridge to the Mediterranean or to undermine our commitments to our truest allies. Seen through this prism, the discussions around the JCPOA can be used as a tool to create and support such a coalition. The same JCPOA that Iran has used as cover to expand its influence can be used to provide cover to a coalition determined to roll them back. It is a function of will and tactics. The Administration has proposed a policy of rollback. It is Congress's duty to go even beyond this and to both hold the Administration's feet to the fire and provide the mechanisms for this policy to be implemented. Only through this strategic reassessment, and a robust collaboration between our executive and legislative branches, can America's honor be restored and its interests be truly served.

Economic Leverage

The key to successfully renegotiating the Iran nuclear deal is the key to any successful negotiation: leverage. And while Iran and some of our international partners aren't eager to reopen negotiations, we still have strong leverage to bring them to the table—economic pressure.

It was economic pressure that led foreign countries to go along with sanctions against Iran in the early 2010s. The Obama administration conducted excellent diplomacy in that regard. However, that diplomacy succeeded because our partners knew that under our diplomatic velvet glove there was an iron fist—that the U.S. was willing to penalize foreign companies that continued to do business with Tehran.

Likewise, economic pressure forced Iran to negotiate seriously. Sanctions contributed to high unemployment and inflation, a decline in GDP, and the collapse of Iran's currency. In short, sanctions convinced the Iranian regime that refusing to negotiate could bring about a popular uprising, threatening the regime.

Ideally, the previous administration would have used our considerable leverage to strike a better deal in the first place, but they did not, and now we are where we are. We do not have as much leverage now as we did then, due to the JCPOA's front-loaded sanctions relief for Tehran (which was a major problem with the agreement to begin with). However, we are in a much better negotiating position now than we likely will be when the deal's restrictions on Iran's nuclear program begin to expire in several years. When the UN restrictions against Iran's conventional weapons and missile programs end—in only a few years—we do not want to look back and say we failed to prevent Iran's further empowerment in the region.

While some foreign companies have struck deals with Tehran, most have stayed away because of the many risks of Iran business—particularly the risk that sanctions will be reimposed. That gives us leverage to urge the Europeans and other countries to join the U.S. in seeking a better deal now, since most of them would not engage in business with Iran at the cost of being excluded from the American market. However, if we choose to forego seeking a better deal now, foreign companies will naturally respond to that signal by rushing to sign contracts with the regime, eliminating any chance of improving the JCPOA later, if only because Iran will use their increased investments as economic hostages to prevent European sanctions.

While Iran's economy has improved greatly since the nuclear deal was signed, that economic growth and stability is still tenuous, and could be sidelined by failure to sign many more lucrative contacts with foreign firms. Tehran also badly wants access to the global financial system. But we also do not want to be in a position where a future increase in oil prices provides

Iran with sufficient revenue which strengthens the regime and funds IRGC efforts.

The Trump administration holds good cards, but it must play them well. And that means not only partnering with our allies but working in lockstep with Congress. The White House must do better in reaching out to both Republicans and Democrats on the Hill to solicit recommendations and gain buy-in for an improved Iran policy.

Next Steps

What, in turn, should the U.S. government—specifically Congress—do to help?

First, the administration should designate the Qods Force as a foreign terrorist organization (FTO). The Trump administration wisely applied more intensive terrorism sanctions to the IRGC, as a whole, under Executive Order 13224, as the Bush administration had done to the Qods Force in 2007. However, the secretary of state retains the discretion to label the Qods Force as an FTO under Section 219 of the Immigration and Nationality Act. In 2009, Kata'ib Hizballah was added as an FTO, and the Qods Force publicly supports them. It's well past time that the Qods Force be similarly designated. Such a step provides the U.S. additional leverage in influencing Iranian and European behavior. Down the line, if Iranian behavior remains unchanged or gets worse, Washington should consider designating the IRGC as a whole as an FTO.

Second, I would note that the public debate over decertification has obscured a more fundamental problem: the absence of a serious, holistic strategy to counter Tehran's non-nuclear destabilizing behavior in the Middle East and beyond. Proponents of the JCPOA argued that it would potentially moderate Iran over time, and that it would make it easier to push back against Iran's multifaceted dangerous behavior by resolving the nuclear issue. Instead, fear of rocking the boat on the nuclear deal deterred the Obama administration and our allies from adequately resisting Iranian regional aggression—which has only increased—even though the JCPOA benefits Tehran far more than it does us. President Rouhani's statement on Monday shows why this is so important. He said, "the greatness of the nation of Iran in the region is more than at any other time… in Iraq, Syria, Lebanon, northern Africa, in the Persian Gulf region — where can action be taken without Iran?"

President Trump wisely laid out the case against Iran's destabilizing non-nuclear conduct, but the administration needs to follow through with the specifics of a comprehensive diplomatic, military, and economic plan to push back against Tehran. Most urgently, the U.S. must work with our allies and others to develop a global consensus—similar to the one that existed before the JCPOA was inked—that the status quo of Iran's destabilizing activities is unacceptable and unsustainable. Responsible nations, in turn, must impose crippling sanctions on Tehran targeting its support for terrorism, regional meddling, and human rights abuses—an approach that would not be inconsistent with the nuclear-related sanctions that were waived under the JCPOA. Congress should hold the Trump administration's feet to the fire to ensure a robust action plan. Indeed, the most vocal supporters of JCPOA speak of the other tools we have to employ against Iran's mischief. Let's use them, and I ask supporters of the JCPOA to stand with us in this campaign.

Third, Congress should pass legislation that reaffirms congressional willingness to reimpose sanctions if the deal is not strengthened to eliminate the sunset clauses, bolster restrictions on Iran's ballistic missile program, including its proliferation of missile technology in the region, and guarantee inspectors enough access to verify that Iran is not violating its commitments.

Fourth, that legislation should preserve the Iran Nuclear Agreement Review Act's requirement that the president recertify Iranian compliance with the deal every 90 days—or at most extend it to every 120 days. The certification process keeps our international partners and Iran on notice and strengthens our leverage by heightening risk awareness by foreign companies considering doing business with Iran (which would diminish U.S. leverage).

Fifth, to maintain public awareness of this issue, Congress should hold regular, quarterly public hearings with senior administration officials to update Congress on the status of efforts to improve the nuclear deal, on the Iranian threat to America, and on how the administration is countering that threat. Twice a year, those hearings should coincide with and focus on the executive branch's issuance of the updated "strategy for deterring conventional and asymmetric Iranian activities and threats" mandated by the Countering America's Adversaries Through Sanctions Act.

Sixth, Congress should direct the president to appoint a special envoy for Iran, who would take the day-to-day lead in engaging diplomatically with other countries. Naming a special envoy—who can speak for the president—would create visibility and draw attention to this issue. The envoy would report directly to the White House, and coordinate efforts across the departments of State, the Treasury, and Energy, as well as the intelligence community. The envoy's mandate would be advancing U.S. interests related to the nuclear and non-nuclear files on Iran.

Seventh, Congress should fully fund the office of the special envoy, as well as Iran-focused efforts within the State Department's Bureau of Near Eastern Affairs, Bureau of Counterterrorism and Countering Violent Extremism, Bureau of International Security and Nonproliferation, and Bureau of Verification and Compliance.

Lastly, Congress should mandate declassification (with a classified annex, if necessary) of the president's semiannual report to Congress pursuant to the Iran Nuclear Agreement Review Act. This report covers Iranian behavior across many areas, including Tehran's nuclear program, ballistic missile program, proliferation of missile technology to proxies, sponsorship of terrorism, and human rights violations. Most importantly, the report must include "[a]ny action or failure to act by Iran that breached the agreement or is in noncompliance [emphasis added] with the terms of the agreement." Declassifying would help to factually rebut claims of Iranian compliance with the JCPOA and draw public attention to Iran's destabilizing activities.

Countering Iranian aggression and improving the JCPOA will be difficult, but not impossible, and they are vital in order to actually prevent a nuclear-armed and emboldened Iran for the long term. If the executive and legislative branches work closely together, the U.S. can use its leverage to get the better nuclear deal we need and roll back the broader Iranian threat. Thank you.

Ms. Ros-Lehtinen. Thank you, Ambassador, and thank you for your testimony, and don't do that again. Thank you. [Laughter.]

Ambassador Wallace. I don't think I have to.

Ms. Ros-Lehtinen. Dr. Gordon, we are so pleased that you are joining us, and we would love to hear from you. Thank you, sir.

STATEMENT OF PHILIP H. GORDON, PH.D., MARY AND DAVID BOIES SENIOR FELLOW IN U.S. FOREIGN POLICY, COUNCIL ON FOREIGN RELATIONS (FORMER WHITE HOUSE COORDINATOR FOR THE MIDDLE EAST, NORTH AFRICA, AND THE GULF REGION)

Mr. Gordon. Thank you for having me, Madam Chairman, Ranking Member Deutch, and all the distinguished members of the committee. I also want to thank you for the honor of being here, and I look forward to the discussion with my two distinguished colleagues.

In my longer written testimony, I discuss, also, a number of ideas for how the United States can not only ensure that Iran never gets a nuclear weapon, but also how we can more effectively respond to Iran's continued support for terrorism, use of proxies to interfere in neighboring states, development of ballistic missiles that threaten, or could threaten, us or Iran's neighbors, and persistent human rights violations which includes, as has been mentioned here, the unjustified and appalling detention of American citizens. And I hope and I am sure we will have a chance to discuss all of those ideas because I think there is a lot we can do that is consistent with the JCPOA and consistent with keeping the support of our allies, both of which I think are important principles.

But I will use my summary oral remarks here to just make my core point, which is my concern that decertification under the Iran Nuclear Agreement Review Act risks collapsing a nuclear deal that is working, isolating the United States, undermining American credibility, and, most importantly, freeing Iran from its nuclear constraints. As has been discussed, we all know President Trump announced on October 13th that he would not certify the Iran nuclear deal according to the terms of INARA, even though the U.S. intelligence community, the International Atomic Energy Agency, our European allies, and numerous Israeli security officials, all concluded that Iran was complying with it. In making that decision, the President has passed near-term responsibility for the issue to Congress, threatening to "terminate," and I quote, the JCPOA if Congress and our allies do not take measures to "address the deal's many serious flaws."

The administration's game plan seems to be to use the threat of walking away from the deal to get Congress and the allies to agree on changes and for Iran back to the table to accept a "better deal." And legislative ideas are circulating about how to do that, including addressing ballistic missiles, access to military sites, and extending the limits on Iran's uranium enrichment.

Now I would be the first to say these are all desirable goals. I don't think anybody would disagree with that. The problem is that the United States cannot unilaterally alter fundamental terms of a deal, and I think it is wishful thinking to imagine that our allies or other parties will agree to do so.

The JCPOA resulted from more than 2 years of difficult multilateral negotiations and has been endorsed by the U.N. Security Council and is supported by virtually every country in the world, including countries like Japan, India, South Korea, and others, whose cooperation with sanctions and cuts in Iranian oil purchases was essential to get the deal in the first place.

Unilaterally amending the provisions of that deal, whether by including new issues or attempting to extend some of its provisions indefinitely, would be considered by all of our allies in Iran violations of the deal, just as we would consider it impermissible for Iran to unilaterally alter its terms. The leaders of Britain, France, and Germany, and the EU have already made clear that they are concerned about the potential implications of the President's decertification, and the EU is already considering activating blocking statutes that would forbid its companies from cooperating with U.S. secondary sanctions.

But, even if our European allies, along with Russia and China, were somehow persuaded to seek changes, it is hard to see how Iran would ever agree to give up now what it would not give up when the international pressure campaign was at its peak. Of course, if our allies in Iran refuse to amend the deal, the United States can always pull out unilaterally, as the President has threatened to do. Indeed, decertification gives Congress the authority to use expedited procedures to reimpose nuclear sanctions for 60 days from the date of the President's announcement. And even if Congress chooses not to do so, the President, as he reminded us, can reimpose those sanctions at anytime. Either of those steps, however, would almost certainly lead to the collapse of the deal.

And all of these scenarios triggered by this decertification decision I think would have serious consequences. They would isolate the United States, leaving it alone to explain why it killed a deal that they believed was working and make it difficult to reassemble that sanctions coalition. It would badly damage the United States' reputation as a reliable partner and diminish our ability to persuade other potential proliferators, including North Korea, that the United States would respect the deal, even if they made painful concessions.

And most importantly, they would free Iran from all the restrictions of the JCPOA, including extensive inspection provisions. If we walk away from the deal, Iran will likely assume its frozen nuclear activities, potentially leaving us with terrible alternatives while acquiescing to their advances or using military force to temporarily set them back. I think this approach is particularly unfortunate because I do believe that JCPOA is doing what it was designed to do, which is prevent Iran from getting a nuclear weapon.

Now I know some Members are concerned about the deal's sunset provisions, which, again, I think we will have a chance to talk about, but remember that, even after some of the deal's restrictions expire on uranium enrichment in 2025 or 2030, Iran is permanently obliged never to seek, develop, or acquire a nuclear weapon, permanently committed never to engage in activities that could contribute to the development of a nuclear explosive device, and will continue to adhere to the IAEA's Additional Protocol, its most comprehensive and intrusive inspections regime. The bottom line is, if we leave the deal today out of concern about sunset provisions, we will effectively be bringing about immediate sunset with no constraints on enrichment, none on research and development, ballistic missiles, or comprehensive inspections.

Let me just end, if I might, with one point about North Korea which has been brought up, and is often brought up, in this context by critics of the JCPOA as a potential reason to pull out of the deal. I actually think the North Korea precedent carries a different message. Not long after the Clinton administration had negotiated an agreement in 1994 to stop North Korea's nuclear program, Congress withdrew support for that agreement, rejecting what it considered to be appeasement of a rogue state and insisting that the Clinton administration negotiate a better deal. In part as a result, we ended up not with a better deal, but with no deal at all, and the nuclear-armed, ballistic-1missile-producing North Korea that we are dealing with today.

We will never know if it would have been possible to effectively implement an agreement with the North Korean regime that we know tried to cheat and may have been determined to seek nuclear weapons, but we do know the result of not trying to do so. And I think Congress and the administration should keep that precedent in mind as they consider whether to risk killing a deal that is working now and rolling the dice that they can produce an even better one.

Madam Chairman, members of the committee, thank you, and I look forward to your questions.

[The prepared statement of Mr. Gordon follows:]

October 25, 2017

The President's Iran Decision: Next Steps

Prepared statement by
Philip H. Gordon
Mary and David Boies Senior Fellow for U.S. Foreign Policy
Council on Foreign Relations

Before the

House Foreign Affairs Subcommittee on the Middle East and North Africa
United States Senate/ United States House of Representatives
1st Session, 115th Congress

Hearing on "The President's Iran Decision: Next Steps"

Madam Chairman, Mr. Ranking Member, and distinguished members of the Committee: Thank you for inviting me to appear before you today to discuss the President's decision to "decertify" the Iran nuclear deal (Joint Comprehensive Plan of Action or JCPOA) and the steps the United States and Congress should take to ensure Iran never acquires a nuclear weapon and to prevent it from threatening the United States and its allies in the region and around the world. There are few more important or urgent issues facing the United States today and I appreciate your inviting me to appear along with two other distinguished experts for a discussion of these critical issues.

The Iranian regime remains implacably hostile to the United States and continues to foment instability in the Middle East through its sponsorship of terrorism and use of proxies to expand its regional influence. It remains a vital U.S. national interest to ensure it never acquires a nuclear weapon while countering its destabilizing activities in the region at the same time.

To help think about how best to achieve these goals and the next steps the United States should take, I will make three main points: 1) the JCPOA is doing what it was designed to do—prevent Iran from advancing toward a nuclear weapons capability; 2) terminating the JCPOA—as the President has threatened to do if it is not amended—would isolate the United States, allow Iran to resume its full range of nuclear activities, and badly undermine U.S. credibility around the world; and 3) the United States can do more to prevent Iran from threatening U.S. interests in the region and around the world, but we will be better placed to do so if we remain in the deal, with the support of our allies, than if we walk away from it.

1) The JCPOA is doing what it was designed to do.

As Congress considers "next steps"—and certainly before it takes any legislative measures that could lead to the deal's termination—it is important to recall where we were before we had the deal and what it has accomplished.[1] By the time negotiations started in 2012, Iran had mastered the full nuclear fuel cycle. It had installed some 19,000 centrifuges, was doing unconstrained centrifuge research and development, and was about to complete the construction of a heavy water reactor that if completed could have produced enough weapons-grade plutonium for up to two bombs per year. It had a stockpile of around 30,000 pounds of low (below 5 percent) enriched uranium, was expanding its stockpile of 20 percent enriched uranium that would have made developing nuclear weapons faster and easier, and there were many open and outstanding questions about its compliance and cooperation with International Atomic Energy Agency inspections.

Today, as a result of the JCPOA (as we know from the additional inspectors and 24/7 cameras that were deployed as part of the deal), Iran operates only some 5,000 older-model centrifuges, maintains a much-reduced stockpile of enriched uranium, limits its centrifuge research and development programs, and has dismantled the core of its heavy water nuclear reactor, which is now filled with concrete. I vividly remember discussions with Israeli national security officials in 2013 about our mutual concerns if that reactor was ever completed—now it never will be. Contrary to what is often alleged by critics, including President Trump last week, Iran had to take all of these steps before it got any sanctions relief. Whereas experts assess that, at the time of the deal, Iran was only months from being able to produce enough nuclear material for a bomb, under these new terms it is now at least a year away, sufficient time for the international community to observe any danger and act accordingly.

I know some Members are concerned about the deal's "sunset" provisions. But remember that even after some of the deal's restrictions expire—in 2025 or 2030—Iran is permanently obliged never to "seek, develop, or acquire" a nuclear weapon, prohibited from doing weaponization work, and will continue to adhere to the IAEA's "Additional Protocol," its most comprehensive and intrusive inspections regime. No country has ever acquired a nuclear weapon while operating under the Additional Protocol, and Iran's obligation to adhere to it never expires. In short, as a result of the JCPOA, we are significantly less vulnerable to Iranian nuclear "breakout" than we would be in its absence, and we will remain so indefinitely—with an improved ability to see any attempted breakout coming and deal with it if it does. Ten, twenty, or thirty years from now, Iran will still be prohibited from undertaking weaponization activities and obliged to provide the IAEA access to its nuclear facilities; without the deal Iran could quickly have a weapons-making capability with none of these restrictions or verification measures in place. The irony of leaving the current deal out of concern about such sunset provisions, of course, is that all the restrictions on Iran would sunset immediately.

---

[1] Some of what follows draws on an article I wrote with Richard Nephew, lead sanctions expert for the U.S. team negotiating with Iran, see Philip Gordon and Richard Nephew, "The 'Worst Deal Ever' that Actually Wasn't," *The Atlantic*, July 14, 2017.

I know many fair-minded critics who point out that their preferred alternative to the JCPOA was not "no deal" but simply a "better deal." I certainly understand and respect that line of thinking and would not argue that the JCPOA is perfect. No arms control agreement—or any international agreement for that matter—ever has been. It is of course possible that the Obama administration and its partners—if they had dragged the negotiations out for even longer than two years or walked away in July 2015—could have gotten more in certain areas from Iran. It is also possible, however, that holding out for more—especially on the questions that critics consider the JCPOA's "fundamental flaws"—could have scuttled any deal entirely. I certainly know of no evidence to support the President's assertion in his decertification speech that Iran was given sanctions relief "just before what would have been the total collapse of the Iranian regime."

Some critics also claim that the threat of force could have forced Iran to make more concessions, but that is also far from guaranteed. There are plenty of cases in recent history—Serbia in 1999, Iraq in 2003, Libya in 2011 just to name a few—where even the credible threat of military force did not lead a dictator to make the concessions we demanded, but instead lead to large, costly, and risky military operations with unintended consequences. This is not to say military force should be ruled out to deal with any Iranian attempt to seek a nuclear weapon today or in the future. On the contrary, the administration should maintain and Congress should fund the necessary military capabilities to keep that threat credible. But we should not imagine that the threat of force alone will get Iran to give us everything we want; threatening force to achieve a perfect agreement could lead to having to use it, with unpredictable consequences.

2) Decertification risks collapsing the deal, undermining American credibility, and freeing Iran from its nuclear constraints.

Understanding the benefits of the deal—and the lack of realistic alternatives—helps to understand why the President's decertification decision puts the United States on such a perilous and unnecessary course. Whereas the U.S. intelligence community, the IAEA, the Europeans, and numerous Israeli security officials all concluded that Iran is complying with the agreement—and the President's own Defense Secretary, General James Mattis, testified that it was in the U.S. interest—President Trump announced on October 13 that he would not certify the deal according to the terms of the Iran Nuclear Agreement Review Act. In so doing, he passed near-term responsibility for the issue to Congress, threatening to "terminate" the JCPOA if Congress and our allies do not take measures to "address the deal's many serious flaws." The administration's game plan seems to be to use the threat of walking away from the deal to get Congress and the allies to agree on changes and force Iran back to the table to accept a "better deal." Legislative ideas are currently circulating to amend the deal to include further restrictions on ballistic missiles, expand weapons inspectors' access to Iranian military sites, and extend the limits on Iran's uranium enrichment and centrifuge research and development capacity indefinitely.

Needless to say, these are all desirable goals. The problem is that it impossible for the United States to unilaterally alter fundamental terms of the deal or to imagine that our allies and other parties will agree to try to do so. The JCPOA resulted from more than two years of difficult, multilateral negotiations, has been endorsed by the UN Security Council, and is supported by virtually the entire international community—including countries like Japan, India, South Korea whose cooperation with sanctions and cuts in oil purchases were essential to getting the deal in the first place. Unilaterally amending the provisions of that deal under these circumstances—whether by including new issues or attempting to extend some of its provisions indefinitely—would be considered by all our allies and Iran as violations of the deal, just as we would consider it impermissible for Iran to unilaterally alter its terms.

Britain, France, Germany and the EU have all already made clear they are concerned about the potential implications of President's decertification decision and stand committed to full implementation of the deal. Indeed, the EU is already considering activating "blocking statues"—adopted in the 1990s to resist U.S. extra-territorial legislation—that would forbid its companies from cooperating with U.S. secondary sanctions and compensate them for possible penalties. But even if our allies, along with Russia and China, were somehow persuaded to try to seek changes, it is hard to see how Iran would ever agree to give up now what it would not give up when the international pressure campaign was at its peak. Instead, Iran would likely respond to any attempt on our part to alter the deal with its own unilateral amendments, eventually leading to the deal's ultimate erosion.

Of course, if our allies and Iran refuse to amend the deal, the United States can always pull out unilaterally—as the President has threatened to do. Indeed "decertification" gives Congress authority to use expedited procedures to re-impose nuclear sanctions for sixty days from the date of the President's announcement, and even if it chooses not to do so, the President can effectively re-impose sanctions himself at any time. Either of those steps, however, would almost certainly lead to the collapse of the deal.

All of these scenarios—triggered by the decertification decision, the failure of an unrealistic renegotiation plan, and the ultimate termination of the deal—would have serious consequences. They would isolate the United States, leaving it alone to explain why it killed a deal they believed was working and making it difficult to re-assemble an effective global sanctions coalition. They would badly damage the United States' reputation as a reliable partner and diminish the U.S. ability to persuade other potential proliferators—including North Korea—that the United States will respect a deal with them even if they make painful concessions. And most importantly, they would free Iran from all the restrictions of the JCPOA, including its extensive inspection provisions. Iran would likely resume its frozen nuclear activities, potentially leaving us with the terrible alternatives of allowing those activities to advance even in the face of sanctions, or using military force to temporarily set them back.

Some critics of the Iran nuclear deal often point to North Korea as the case against "flawed" agreements. But the North Korea precedent actually carries a different message. Not long after the Clinton administration had negotiated an agreement in 1994 to stop Pyongyang's nuclear program, Congress withdrew support for that agreement, rejecting what it considered the "appeasement" of a rogue state and insisting that the Clinton administration negotiate a "better deal." In part as a result, we ended up not with a better deal but with no deal at all — and the paranoid, nuclear-armed North Korea that we are dealing with today. We will never know if it would have been possible to effectively implement an agreement with a North Korean regime that we know tried to cheat and may have been determined to seek nuclear weapons, but we do know the result of not trying to do so. Congress and the administration should keep that precedent in mind as they consider whether to risk killing a deal that is working and rolling the dice that they can produce an even better one.

3) We Can Enforce the JCPOA and Counter Iran at the Same Time.

Even while fully complying with the JCPOA, the United States can do more to vigorously confront Iran's many other threats to U.S. interests and partners. Indeed, the deal's negotiators were very clear with Congress, our allies, and the Iranians, that we would not hesitate to stand up to Iran in the region and penalize its continued support for terrorism, use of proxies to interfere in neighboring states, development of ballistic missiles that could threaten us or Iran's neighbors, and persistent human rights violations (which includes the unjustified and appalling detention of American citizens). We should do just that, while understanding there is a far better chance of achieving our goals if the United States pursues them while maintaining the support of our allies and making Iran's behavior—rather than American trustworthiness—the focus of international attention. Iran's leaders like nothing more than seeing Americans divided among themselves and separated from their key international partners.

Looking ahead, there are several things the United States can do both to counter the spread of Iranian influence in the region and to ensure that the JCPOA works effectively not just now but even after some of its restrictions are lifted.

The first step is to fully enforce the current deal in all its aspects. Contrary to what some critics allege, the deal includes effective enforcement provisions including the ability for the United States to force the re-imposition of UN sanctions in case Iran violates key provisions and fails to remedy the violation according to the processes provided for in the deal. The main Iranian "violation" of the deal cited on October 13 by President Trump—its temporary possession of slightly more than its limit of 130 metric tons of heavy water—was actually an excellent example of the effective functioning of the deal. The excess was quickly observed by inspectors and Iran quickly remedied the situation (which in any case was not threatening because the JCPOA had already required Iran to dismantle its only heavy water reactor and has no reprocessing capacity). Nor is it accurate that the JCPOA does not provide access to Iranian military sites. If there is a basis for such access Iran must provide it; our chances of reaching agreement with our partners and the IAEA on that basis will be greater if we abide by the deal ourselves rather than convey the impression that we are looking for a pretext to blow it up.

Second, we should use all the tools at our disposal—including the full range of sanctions consistent with the JCPOA—to increase the costs for Iranian support for terrorism, ballistic missile activity, and human rights violations. Congress took a useful step in this direction last summer with the sanctions authorized in the Countering America's Adversaries Through Sanctions Act, which the administration has for some reason been slow in implementing. We should also do more to empower local actors in Iraq, Syria, Yemen, and elsewhere who are attempting to resist Iran's efforts to exercise control. We should pursue discussions with our European allies about complementary steps they could take, including designating the entirety of Hezbollah as a terrorist group, sanctioning entities for ballistic missile work, and cutting off money flowing to Iranian front companies and logistics pipelines involved in proliferation or terrorism. At the same time we should understand that efforts to pressure them into some of these steps by threatening to terminate the JCPOA or with secondary sanctions could backfire; some European officials have already said such steps have become more difficult now that the President has made European support a prerequisite for remaining in the nuclear deal.

Third, the United States can counter Iran by continuing to provide vigorous support to our allies and partners in the region most vulnerable to Iranian meddling. This support should include implementation of the 2016 ten-year Memorandum of Understanding to provide an unprecedented $38 billion over 10 years to Israel—including $5 billion for missile defense assistance and resources for additional F-35 aircraft—as well as continued defense sales and missile defense cooperation with our Gulf partners. Congressional approval of the sale of the Terminal High-Altitude Area Defense system to Saudi Arabia will send a strong message that the United States will act to counter the expansion of Iran's ballistic missile program. Iran's regional neighbors collectively already spend many times more on defense and security than Tehran; we should ensure that they continue to have the means necessary to defend themselves and deter further Iranian encroachment.

I know many Members of Congress have legitimate concerns that the sanctions relief provided to Iran as part of the JCPOA has fueled Iran's expansion throughout the region, the reality is that Tehran's interference in the domestic affairs of regional states is relatively cheap, and relatively insensitive to Iran's overall budgetary picture. While a boost in revenues from unfrozen assets and increased oil sales obviously provides some scope for military interventionism, the director of the Defense Intelligence Agency has testified that the "preponderance" of those assets have gone to economic development and infrastructure, as one would expect given Iran's enormous domestic needs. And the idea that a windfall from sanctions relief has turned Iran into an economic powerhouse fails to take into account the degree to the collapse in oil prices have undercut much of the financial benefit Iran has received.

Fourth, the United States should do more to reenergize diplomacy in the region, to contain the conflicts—in Syria, Yemen, Iraq and elsewhere—that Iran exacerbates and exploits to expand its influence. An underfunded and demoralized State Department—where key positions remain unfilled—doesn't help. Nine months into the administration we still have no ambassador in Qatar or Saudi Arabia and not even a nominee for the critical position of Assistant Secretary of State for Near Eastern Affairs.

Finally, looking even further ahead, the administration could start discussions now with our allies about potential supplementary or follow-on agreements to the JCPOA. Such discussions might explore the possibility of extending the duration of certain nuclear restrictions, or arrangements by which Iran would rely on an international consortium for enriched uranium rather than developing an industrial-scale national program. Like the JCPOA itself, these outcomes could only result from give-and-take among the parties and the United States would have to put something on the table, but the potential trade-offs are worth exploring. By staying in the JCPOA and demonstrating that we uphold our end of an agreement when we reach one, we will be better placed to hold our adversaries to this and potentially other such agreements in the future.

Madam Chairman and Members of the Committee, the JCPOA has certainly not solved all of our problems with Iran, which will require constant focused attention and resources going forward. If we confront these challenges on a strong, bipartisan basis, and with the support of our key allies abroad, I am confident they can be met.

Thank you for inviting me and I look forward to responding to your questions.

Ms. ROS-LEHTINEN. Thank you very much, Dr. Gordon. Thank you for joining us.

And thanks, all of you, for your testimony. Clearly, we have a lot to address here.

Dr. Heinonen, I would like to start with you. I wanted to touch on an issue you raised in your testimony and an issue we heard 2 weeks ago, also, from David Albright when he testified before our full committee. And that is regarding Iran's likely violations of some of the conditions of Section T. Could you tell us why you believe Iran is likely in violation of Section T, why the IAEA would require access to military sites for its verification, and why IAEA access to military sites in general is critical to being able to certify and verify the JCPOA?

Mr. HEINONEN. Thank you, Chairman Ros-Lehtinen.

When I look at Section T, and I look at the conclusions of the IAEA report, I cannot read the report in such a way that the IAEA states that Iran is in whole compliance with its obligations under Section T. Why do I say so? Because what the IAEA addresses, that it is monitoring and verifying Section T. It doesn't tell, like we used to say in 2003 when we had the EU 3 agreement, where the centers continued and said there is no indication that Iran is in noncompliance with this undertaking. So, the IAEA leaves this a little bit open in the text, and this is why I request or suggest that the text should be more precise. Tell us, is Iran fully complying?

Then comes the second part of this exercise, which was also erased. It is when the IAEA says that it verifies Section T, at the same time the IAEA Secretary insists that they have never visited during this implementation period any military sites. So, it is difficult to understand which kind of methodology the IAEA uses to monitor, for example, these multi-point detonation systems, which certain types of them are proscribed under Section T. So, how can the IAEA come to the conclusion that such activities don't exist? Or is it actually that the IAEA has not been yet able to verify?

So, therefore, it is important that the IAEA comes out and tells us if there is a problem and, then, addresses the problem and has those accesses and tells us what exactly has been done. And this, I think, is very important to the creating of the reports and critical to the verification system. There should be no limitations on accessing those places because Section T is an obligation for Iran to implement.

Ms. ROS-LEHTINEN. That is very clear. Thank you so much.

Ambassador Wallace, you state that the key piece of leverage that we have on Iran is economic pressure. As I mentioned, our European friends—and you have mentioned it as well—have entered into many deals with Iran worth billions of dollars. In other words, they have significant economic interest in Iran. They have not taken any action against Iran on anything non-nuclear-related, partly because they don't want to damage their economic opportunities in Tehran. And as you noted, we don't have the leverage now that we had previously over Iran, but we have leverage with the EU to seek a better deal.

So, I ask you, how do we leverage this opportunity now to get the EU to both work with us to get a better deal and to take serious action against Iran's non-nuclear-related activity?

Ambassador WALLACE. Thank you, Madam Chairman.

Look, this committee and the group of people that worked in the Iran space became expert at applying economic pressure to bring Iran to the table and to influence their economy. The charts that we have provided here show economic data associated with the time of sanctions before, during, and after the JCPOA. And you can see the effect that you all had and the administration had related to Iran. We have to get back to that place.

And I would assert that, as Iran has used the JCPOA to promote its activities, they have used the cover of the JCPOA as if everything else is hands-off. We can use our concerns about the JCPOA and our concerns about Iran's behavior to drive the leverage to impose additional economic pressure on Iran.

Mr. Deutch, Chairman Ros-Lehtinen, you all have done this for years, and that is, frankly, what led to the JCPOA. And I would just say we have to take a deep breath about the decertification issue. We have a lot of fake debates in Washington these days, and I would suggest that, with due respect, the decertification was a little of a fake debate. The sky didn't fall with certification or not certification. Now we have to deal with Iran's behavior. As Iran did not deal, and our Government did not want to include a variety of issues in its negotiations in the JCPOA, it carved out everything from missiles to terrorism, to human rights.

Let's now readdress those. Let's respect the JCPOA as best as we can. Let's use our allies and our mutual concerns about Iran's behavior and our mutual concerns about the JCPOA, and the continuing leverage that we have and that you all can provide, by enacting ever-increasing economic pressure to drive supplemental agreements or other pushback of Iran, such as, as Secretary Tillerson said the other day, why are the Shia militia still in Iraq? We effectively allowed them to digest Iraq like a python eating prey.

We have to push Iran back, and we have to use our economic pressure to do that. It has worked in the past; it can work again, but it requires a bipartisan consensus. And this committee has always been able to do that.

Ms. ROS-LEHTINEN. Thank you very much for that thoughtful response.

And Mr. Deutch has opted to be the closer. So, we will turn to Mr. Schneider.

Mr. SCHNEIDER. Thank you and, again, thank you for holding this very important hearing.

To the witnesses, thank you for your insight and sharing your perspectives.

Ambassador Wallace, I want to start with you. In your submitted testimony, one of the things you talk about is, and I will quote you, "the absence of a serious holistic strategy to counter Tehran's non-nuclear destabilizing behavior in the Middle East and beyond." And you lay out a number of steps here, but, more broadly—and I will open this to everyone—what are the dynamics of the absence of that strategy right now? Why is it so important that the United States articulate a clear and comprehensive strategy?

Ambassador WALLACE. Look, I read everyone's statements as part of my preparation for this. Congressman Deutch, I read yours.

I agreed with almost everything that you said. And one of the things that you said—in answer to Congressman Schneider—was that we have always sort of had a holistic strategy as part of our approach. What was good, I think, about the President's statement is he outlined all of Iran's other behavior and we have to begin to push back on that behavior, and we can do that through economic pressure.

It is not clear to me that that has ever been laid out. Look, I fault the administration under which I served for not laying that out more deliberately. I give some fault to President Obama and his team for not laying that more deliberately. I don't think it was as effectively laid out.

This committee, in my opinion, gets it because you have been enacting most of the legislation about it. But, when you look at that holistic strategy from their adventurism around the region, from their support of terrorism, their testing of ballistic missiles, certainly the less good of provisions of the JCPOA, we can use the tools of legislation, the tools of Treasury sanctions, the tools of State Department sanctions, including the foreign terrorist organizations.

It is all about risk. I have talked to these companies. We talk to them, thousands of them. They are averse to risk. We have to explain to them that the risk of doing business in Iran because of its intransigent behavior in the region is too great to go there. If Western businesses flood into Iran to support an IRGC-dominated economy, God forbid we are ever in a circumstance like North Korea, for whatever reason; we will have a much harder time, God forbid, threatening a military intervention, which no one wants, if a bunch of Western businesses and interests are there. So, that is why it is important to act and deal with all the issues that were not dealt with during the JCPOA.

Mr. SCHNEIDER. And to expand, maybe I will turn to you, Dr. Heinonen, because you touched on this. The urgency to act now, it is not by ripping apart the JCPOA, if I understand what you are saying, Ambassador. It is doing everything around the JCPOA and picking up the pieces that weren't addressed by the narrow nuclear focus on the JCPOA. Is that a correct interpretation?

Ambassador WALLACE. Sorry, Olli.

Mr. HEINONEN. Yes, sir, to the greatest extent. There are authorities which the IAEA Board of Governors has, like asking for more detailed reporting. It has nothing to do with the JCPOA. It is in the normal practices which the IAEA Board of Governors has exercised for years, and that is just a simple resolution by the Board. Due to the IAEA Board practices, there is also no legal right. So, I think that this is an elegant way to get better enforcement and better reporting.

Then, missile issues might be different because they fall to the domain of the U.N. Security Council, but there are ways and means to change the course without renegotiating every aspect of the JCPOA. And also, the Joint Committee has certain leverage and certain flexibility to do interpretations, particularly when it comes, for example, to breakout times and constraints there.

Mr. SCHNEIDER. And how are we best positioned to make sure that the breakout time, as the various sunsets of the JCPOA fall into place, that the breakout time stays at that 1-year mark, that it doesn't move closer?

Mr. HEINONEN. This means, actually, as I said in my opening statement, continuous followup of the developments in Iran. When we see that they are developing better and faster centrifuges, then we need to access the conditions, that they don't expand the number of installed centrifuges more than what is required for 1-year breakout time, which in technical terms is about 5,000 of those installed.

Mr. SCHNEIDER. I am running out of time, but to emphasize, that is 5,000 of generation 1 centrifuges. As they work on their R&D and move into the next generations, that number has to fall. Otherwise, they are going to have 5,000 faster, more efficient, which will shrink the time.

Mr. HEINONEN. Yes. Thank you. Yes, that is true; once you have this next generation IR-2m, it is only a quarter of that number of centrifuges will be permitted. But, then, comes to the picture another aspect which the people perhaps have not followed thoroughly through. It is that you can manufacture these more efficient centrifuges, stock them, and install them quickly. And this one was not as a part of the declaration.

And as I said in my opening remarks, also, the other part is that I don't think the people would do much thinking how we are going to catch if Iran decides to cheat the system by having a clandestine production of those centrifuges. I think the provisions to that end are weak. And therefore, you need to have some buffer in your breakout time to overcome that problem.

Mr. SCHNEIDER. Thank you. I am out of time, but just to reiterate what the ranking member said, that highlighting Iran's malign activities, past and present, and currently ongoing, even in the context of the JCPOA, I think the time to act and move forward to close those gaps, reduce those risks, is right now.

With that, I yield back.

Ms. ROS-LEHTINEN. Thank you, Mr. Schneider.

Mr. Ron DeSantis of Florida.

Mr. DESANTIS. Thank you.

Ambassador Wallace, looking at some of the reaction to the President's decertification, you saw some of our partners in Europe, you know, resounding endorsements of the JCPOA. But, then, you look at places in the Gulf, Israel, the UAE, I mean, they were happy that the President is taking a different course. It just seems to me that our European allies don't face the same threat from Iran as our Middle Eastern allies, and they have a lot of opportunities for business with Iran. And so, I guess as we go forward, I think it is good to have as many people on the same page as possible, but how do we get them to be more in line with the American perspective, the Israeli perspective, the Middle East perspective of people that are actually threatened by Iran?

Ambassador WALLACE. Thank you, Congressman.

Look, it is a very good point. I would say that we tend to gloss over some of the statements of our P5+1 colleagues that have been favorable. For example, Emmanuel Macron, the new leader in France, has said some very strong and encouraging things regarding Iran's behavior and seems prepared to take action to work with us to push back on other areas of Iran's bad behavior.

So, as Iran has used this agreement to expand its relevance, its importance, and its destabilizing behavior, with respect, I think the administration can wisely use a bit of our threat of being dissatisfied, not international interests, and eventually pulling out of the agreement, to work with our allies like President Macron and our Gulf allies to come up with a good plan to push Iran back in other areas and perhaps to have supplemental understandings about some of the weaknesses of the agreement, perhaps in supplemental agreements.

Mr. DeSantis. Now the EU, they were pretty open in saying, look, if there are other malign activities when the JCPOA was agreed upon, look, we are willing to take actions. But have they taken any action since that has happened?

Ambassador Wallace. No, and I fully agree with you. But I think that there has been a bit of an absence of leadership with the transition of power. And hopefully, we are seeing that here in the United States and in some of the European governments.

And I would just say that the statements out of France are quite encouraging. If I had any say in it, I would say let's immediately reach out to our French colleagues and come up with a plan, so that the Iranians don't have bases on the Mediterranean and the Bab-el-Mandeb.

Mr. DeSantis. Dr. Heinonen, it is frustrating when I hear about Iran complying because we don't have access to all of their sites. I mean, can we get access to some of their military sites if we want to do a prompt inspection?

Mr. Heinonen. Under the provisions of the Safeguards Agreement, this is possible. All territory of Iran is subject to the IAEA safeguards. This is what Iran signed to when it signed the Comprehensive Safeguards Agreement with the IAEA, and, also, the provisions of Additional Protocol cover the whole country.

So, what is needed, then, that the IAEA exercises fully its right? It certainly has to have a reason to go. As I listed in my testimony, there are several reasons why one should go to certain military sites, for example, in Iran to certify, on the one hand, that there is no undeclared nuclear activities going on and there are no undeclared nuclear-weapons-related activities going on. So, the rights are there.

Mr. DeSantis. But we are not in a position; we cannot declare that because we just haven't gone in, right?

Mr. Heinonen. I read, indeed, the IAEA report differently. For me, the wording which is there doesn't state that Iran has fully complied with its obligations, the way I read it. I would like to see, as I said before, some additional language to certify that the IAEA has really verified all aspects of the JCPOA and the Comprehensive Safeguards Agreement.

Mr. DeSantis. Have you made recommendations about dealing with Iran's ballistic missile program?

Mr. Heinonen. Yes. Actually, there are two aspects to that. First of all, when we think nuclear weapons program—and, look at North Korea as an example, this is like a tent with two posts. You need a delivery vehicular-assisted missile and, then, you need the nuclear weapon and the nuclear material itself. And they go hand-by-hand in tandem.

Therefore, when the breakout times get shorter over the time, we need to have more constraints on the missile program to make sure that Iran doesn't dash to nuclear weapon capability. And the only way and means, in my view, to do it is to limit, first of all, the range of missiles, include, also, cruise missiles like we are including in North Korea, but for some reason not in Iran. And then, perhaps to reduce the payload capacity of those missiles and make them less offensive and more defensive in nature.

Mr. DeSantis. Great. Well, obviously, that should have been a part of these negotiations from the beginning, and that was put aside at the very, very outset. And I think it was a huge mistake.

I yield back.

Ms. Ros-Lehtinen. Thank you, Mr. DeSantis.

Mr. Cicilline.

Mr. Cicilline. Thank you, Madam Chairman.

Ambassador Wallace, there are many members of this committee who have expressed deep concern about the hollowing-out of diplomatic posts, and that includes many ambassadorships and assistant secretary positions, and what impact that is having on our diplomatic engagement, coupled with conflicting messages between the President of the United States and his Secretary of State, and sometimes even deferring to the U.N. Ambassador.

And I am wondering whether you could speak to what this sort of disorder, what kind of impact it is having on our Iran policy, and specifically, the kind of confusion that it is creating, what that means in terms of our partners or even our adversaries.

Ambassador Wallace. It is bad, I agree with you. You should fund and staff those departments. In the interim, our strategic confusion, we should try to take advantage of.

Mr. Cicilline. What do you mean by that?

Ambassador Wallace. I think that our policy does appear to be confused, but I think that the power of this—and it is not good, I agreed with you.

Mr. Cicilline. But strategic confusion makes it sound like you think it is actually a strategy that was——

Ambassador Wallace. I don't know.

Mr. Cicilline. Okay.

Ambassador Wallace. You are asking me to interpret something that I can't interpret. But what I can say is that——

Mr. Cicilline. I think that is actually exactly the point.

Ambassador Wallace. Right, but my point is that, don't get bogged down in that. You all can use that confusion strategically——

Mr. Cicilline. Yes.

Ambassador Wallace [continuing]. To advance a narrative to put pressure on and seek good work with our allies.

Mr. Cicilline. Yes. I think it is kind of a frightening idea of don't get bogged down with confusion for the administration on what their approach is.

Dr. Gordon, maybe can you respond to that? Do you think that is a——

Ambassador WALLACE. I just want to respond to that. I don't speak with the administration.

Mr. CICILLINE. I have limited time. Ambassador?

Ambassador WALLACE. I don't speak for the administration.

Mr. CICILLINE. I understand that, but I am just saying that was your argument. I think that is kind of an alarming suggestion, frankly.

Mr. GORDON. Congressman, I think it is deeply damaging in a number of ways. Even among our partners and allies, we don't have an Ambassador in Saudi Arabia; we don't have an Ambassador in Qatar. We don't have an Assistant Secretary of State for Near Eastern Affairs, or even a nominee. And we are trying to manage disputes among those critical partners who are vital to containing Iran. So, it is damaging in that sense.

It is also damaging, if you think about it, whether you want, like I do, to find things we can do with allies consistent with the JCPOA, or whether you want to renegotiate it. You need people to do those things. You need experts and sanctions experts and technical experts and scientists and diplomats. And so, even if somehow our threat to pull out of the deal gets people to agree to talk on what the Europeans can do and what their Gulf friends can do and what Israel can do, you need effective diplomats who can follow up.

Mr. CICILLINE. Thank you, Doctor.

Dr. Heinonen—and I hope I am pronouncing that correctly—as Mr. Deutch mentioned, Monday marked the 34th anniversary of the Beirut bombings. In my home state we lost nine Rhode Islanders in those bombings and we commemorate that every year. And so, I would like to ask you, as we think about Hezbollah's continued global terrorism, support for the Assad regime, their nefarious activities in Lebanon, their stated aim to destroy the State of Israel, how can we, what can we do to best sever the ties between Iran and Hezbollah and around support for Hezbollah? What can and should we be doing?

Mr. HEINONEN. Sir, thank you very much for the question. This goes a little bit beyond my scope. So, I think that maybe Dr. Wallace wants to address that.

But I have been spending the last 20 years of my time in the Middle East and I have been seeing this coming. I see it as a very disturbing factor. In particular, if it turns out that at one point of time Iran also has nuclear weapons capability or is a threshold state with a very short dash to nuclear weapons capability, those problems which we see here now in terms of terrorism and behavior in the region get even more serious. This is the only thing, in my view, which I can state to this topic.

Mr. CICILLINE. Ambassador Wallace, do you have thoughts?

Ambassador WALLACE. Let's sanction the Quds Force. Let's designate them a foreign terrorist organization. The Quds Force is generally—it is more complicated than that—the vehicle under which Iran provides support and largesse, and vice versa, to the Hezbollah. Let's take that step. It is controversial? I don't think it is. I think we should begin about designating the IRGC as a foreign terrorist organization. I think some of our allies would have some heartburn about that because the IRGC technically runs the military of Iran, and it would be the first time that we had taken such an action. But I advocate that we should consider that. We should debate that and have that on the table. That should be part of the ever-increasing consideration of sanctions.

But today, right now, let's designate the Quds Force as an FTO and Qasem Soleimani as its head, and let's start pressuring and convincing companies and businesses around the world that, if you do business that touches on the IRGC and its Quds Force, that you run the risk of doing business with a foreign terrorist organization. That would provide quite a chill, in my opinion, at least a first step of a good freeze.

Mr. CICILLINE. Thank you very much.

I yield back, Madam Chairman.

Ms. ROS-LEHTINEN. Thank you very much, Mr. Cicilline.

And I am so pleased to yield to my Florida colleague, Mr. Mast.

Mr. MAST. Thank you very much, Chairman.

I want to look at a different side of the Joint Comprehensive Plan of Action. It has been readily available for everybody to see, especially in the past week, how the Obama administration, Hillary Clinton, the Clinton Foundation have all worked to sell uranium to Russia. I would personally call it proliferation. So, I want to go with a few questions related to that.

Would you say—and this is open to any one of you—that the JCPOA does allow for Russia to expand its ties with Iran?

Ambassador WALLACE. I think one of the problems with the JCPOA—and we have to remember, the JCPOA, 58 Senators were generally, even though we didn't have the vote on it, were not in support of the JCPOA. I think it was 269 or 270 Members in a bipartisan manner.

And the JCPOA, one of the criticisms at the time—and it did have strings—was that it really was a narrowly-constructed nuclear nonproliferation agreement plus a little bit more. It didn't touch on issues like that, Congressman, and I think that was one of the problems that we had and that was one of the issues that we had, that Iran is—the first trip that representatives of Iran made after signing the JCPOA, in my opinion, was to Moscow, because they were looking for allies in the region, whether it be Syria or otherwise. So, I think that is one of the weaknesses that you identify and you are absolutely right, that is a problem.

Mr. MAST. It was stated by the Russian Foreign Ministry that the deal was based upon what was articulated specifically by Vladimir Putin. That was a quote from the Russian Foreign Ministry after the deal was brought about.

I would like to ask you, as part of the JCPOA, did it lift sanctions on Russian sellers of illicit munitions, illicit arms? Was that part of the JCPOA?

Mr. GORDON. Did it lift sanctions on Russian sales of illicit arms? It provided a pathway to lifting a U.N. Security Council resolution on arms sales to Iran, which was implemented in the context of U.S. leadership bringing the world together to deal with this particular set of issues.

And having been involved in the negotiations, I can tell you that all of these things were desired by the United States. We would, obviously, have loved to have a deal that prevented arms sales to

Iran forever. That included ballistic missiles. That included Iranian intervention in the region.

But you have to remember that the reason we were able to get this international sanctions coalition into place is that we were able to forge a consensus that, remarkably, in fact, even included Russia, to deal with the nuclear threat, which was the prominent issue of most concern to us and everybody else involved.

Mr. MAST. Does Russia build and operate reactors in Iran?

Mr. GORDON. There is one Russian-built and -operated reactor at Bushehr and, then, Russia takes the spent fuel and ensures that it is not a proliferation risk.

Mr. MAST. Is part of the deal that it allows shipments of uranium from Iran to Russia?

Mr. GORDON. Well, when Iran got rid of 97 percent of its uranium stockpile, part of that process was getting rid of that uranium and sending it to Russia, which we thought was a positive thing.

Mr. MAST. So now, Russia is acquiring both the uranium of Iran and the United States of America?

Mr. GORDON. Russia is a nuclear weapons state which has lots and lots of uranium and enriched uranium. And again, we thought it was a better thing to have Iran's stockpile of enriched uranium in Russia, which has more than enough uranium, than in Iran. So, that was an important positive part of the agreement.

Mr. MAST. From one known adversary to another. Would you say that this deal, the Joint Comprehensive Plan of Action, brings Iran closer to the West or closer to Russia?

Mr. GORDON. I don't think it necessarily brings Iran closer to the West because that wasn't the point of the deal. The point of the deal was to ensure that Iran, which when the deal was negotiated was on the verge of a potential weapons capability—we assessed a couple of months away from having enough fissile material for a bomb—the deal was designed to deal with that. And if we had a way to also make it less of an adversary—and again, I think we will come back to, and I have already discussed, some of the many other ways in which Iran is a threat to the United States—but the deal wasn't designed to bring Iran closer to the West. It was designed to deal with the nuclear threat.

Mr. MAST. I thank you for your answers. I think that is always an issue when we have deals that we are bringing about that do not benefit the United States in a way that I think most of us would like to see. Thank you.

Ms. ROS-LEHTINEN. Thank you so much, Mr. Mast.

And now, we turn to Mr. Lieu of California.

Mr. LIEU. Thank you, Madam Chair.

I want to thank the witnesses for your time and your testimony today.

I want to follow on the comments from the gentleman from Florida. I am pleased to see there is bipartisan recognition that Russia is not our ally and Vladimir Putin is not our friend. I hope my colleagues across the aisle will contact the President of the United States and ask him why he blew off a deadline to impose sanctions on Russia, especially after Congress passed a bipartisan law on sanctions.

Now I would like to ask about your comments, Mr. Ambassador, about strategic confusion. What you call strategic confusion I call total and utter dysfunction at the highest levels of the Trump administration when it comes to foreign policy.

Specifically to the Iran deal, we see that the President says that he wants to get out of the Iran deal. In fact, when he campaigned, he said he was going to rip up the deal. At the same time, we have Secretary of Defense Mattis saying it is in the best interest of the United States to stay in the deal. We have Secretary of State Tillerson saying it is in the best interest of the United States to stay in the deal. So, today, on Wednesday, October 25th, I have a very simple and basic question. What is the official policy of the Trump administration on the Iran deal? Do they want to get in or stay in or do they want to get out?

Ambassador WALLACE. If you think you have got the guy here that is going to try to defend that, you are wrong. And no matter the number of Bibles I am going to swear on, I don't have an answer for you. So, you can pass it to somebody else.

Mr. LIEU. All right.

Ambassador WALLACE. I don't speak for the administration.

Mr. LIEU. Any other members of the panel, can you explain the official policy of the Trump administration, as we sit here today? It is a very simple question.

Ambassador WALLACE. I think Phil should take it. [Laughter.]

Mr. LIEU. I mean, if you can't, that is fine. Just say you can't explain it. I get that. I can't.

Mr. GORDON. I don't speak for the Trump administration. Do you mean broadly? I mean, as I articulated, my——

Mr. LIEU. We are reading the same Twitter account. We are reading the same statements from the same Secretaries. So, I just want your view as experts. What is the Trump administration's policy?

Mr. GORDON. I don't know what you are asking me. Broadly policy or toward this decertification?

Mr. LIEU. Towards this Iran deal. What is their official position?

Mr. GORDON. Well, as I said in my opening statement, my understanding of their game plan is to threaten to leave it, to force Congress and allies to agree to change it. And I expressed my own skepticism if that is possible and my concerns that that game plan, while I think the Ambassador is right that in the short-term the sky is not falling, and there is no reason to believe the deal collapses immediately because of that step, I worry that is has set in place a process that could lead to the collapse of the deal with nothing in place to follow it. So, I am very worried about it.

Mr. LIEU. Doctor, do you have—I am just curious about your view as an expert, if you know what the Trump administration's official policy is on the Iran deal, as we sit here today.

Mr. HEINONEN. The way I read this piece is it was a long time in a painful mission on the IAEA. My conclusion is that the United States of America's Government is reviewing the situation and is looking forward what to do, and to that extent, has also asked the opinion of the Congress.

Mr. LIEU. Thank you.

So, let me tell you why strategic confusion, or as I call it, total utter dysfunction, is harmful to the United States. It makes it very confusing to the American public, to Members of Congress, to you on the panel, to world leaders, to understand what our strategy is, what our policy is. And moreover, it totally undercuts the credibility of Secretary of State Rex Tillerson. So, when Secretary of State Tillerson now talks to Members of Congress, if he were to talk to you, if he were to talk to world leaders, we don't actually know who he is speaking for. Is he speaking for himself? Is he speaking for the President? What policy is he advocating that has any support behind it? And that causes massive problems. It makes it very hard to engage in diplomacy.

And the dysfunction also has resulted in numerous positions not being filled. I know that the vacancy for their Assistant Secretary for International Security and Nonproliferation has not been filled. Do you know, as of today, has the President nominated anyone yet for that post? It is a yes-or-no or you don't know. Anyone on the panel? I don't think he has. I think that is a problem, and I hope you would agree that that probably is a pretty important position if we are dealing with nuclear nonproliferation issues.

So, it is my hope that this administration gets its act together. And for anyone who believes strategy incompetence and confusion is good, I just have one rhetorical thought experiment. Think for yourself, would any of you have wanted unpredictability, confusion, or dysfunction during the Cuban Missile Crisis?

I yield back.

Ms. ROS-LEHTINEN. Thank you, Mr. Lieu.

And now, I am pleased to yield to Mr. Fitzpatrick of Pennsylvania.

Mr. FITZPATRICK. Thank you, Madam Chair.

And thank you to the panel for participating.

I have made my views on the JCPOA very clear in this committee. To inject $150 billion in previously-frozen assets into the Iranian economy and the lifting of sanctions, which by most measures will allow that economy to grow at a clip of 10 to 12 percent per year to what most of us would agree is the world's largest state sponsor of terrorism. No anytime anywhere inspections, an agreement that has not been signed by a single government official in Tehran, not a single member of the Iranian Parliament. Violating the spirit of the agreement at best on a regular basis through its ongoing support of regional proxies and/or ongoing ballistic missile tests. So, given all of those factors, my question is, does our faith in this agreement depend upon our belief in the credibility in the Iranian regime that they are going to keep their word?

Mr. GORDON. I would say a couple of things. First, no, it doesn't rely on trust that they will keep their word. It relies on enforcement. I think you have to assume, because they have cheated in the past, that they are capable of cheating again. So, I don't think it is matter of trusting, and that is why the extensive inspections regime that they are committed to forever. We talked about sunsets. One thing that wouldn't sunset was the intrusive inspection regime to assure that they can never get a nuclear weapon. So, I guess, no, it doesn't. It doesn't.

Ambassador WALLACE. If I may just slightly disagree with that, I think that any agreement of this sort requires trust. And we have heard statements that they won't allow inspections of military facilities. We are relying on the Additional Protocol down the road. And to say that, with all due respect to my friend Olli, that inspections are the absolute panacea, I think is wrong, just because, with due respect, I don't think there has ever been an inspections regime that has truly prevented a power from going nuclear if that power wanted to go nuclear.

Mr. GORDON. When we talk about imperfections of the inspection regime, we have to compare it to the inspection regime that we would have in the absence of the JCPOA, in the absence of the Additional Protocol. In fact, no country operating under the Additional Protocol has ever gotten nuclear weapons. And keep in mind that, if we were to say this inspection regime is imperfect and, therefore, we don't like the JCPOA, we would go from this inspection regime with additional monitors, 24/7 cameras on declared nuclear sites, and the ability to access even military bases, if there is a basis for it, we would go from that regime to no regime whatever, kind of like the one we have had in North Korea for 20 years. And that is the case for the JCPOA.

Mr. FITZPATRICK. Mr. Gordon, with all respect, how are we not relying on the credibility of the regime to enforce an agreement that does not allow for anytime anywhere inspections? How is there not an element of us being forced to put our faith in that regime for this agreement to work?

Mr. GORDON. Well, because we are monitoring it. I mean, I think the anytime anywhere is sometimes the wrong standard to think about. I mean, the idea, once again, would we like to have American intelligence personnel on Iranian military bases 24/7? I think, of course, we would, but that has never existed. Other than in the context of a defeated power and occupation, that has never happened and will not happen, and I don't think any of us believe that could be the standard in Iran.

What was important, and remains important, is that, if we have a basis for suspecting that they are not living up to their obligations, not only not to acquire a nuclear weapon, but not even to seek or develop or do R&D on weaponization activities, if we have any basis for that, then we need access to those bases, and have it. And as Olli said, the inspection regime provides for that.

I actually think we have a better chance of getting that—and if not, we have a crisis and, then, all of the means are available, just as if we didn't have the agreement. I think we have a better chance of getting that access if we are living up to the regime, the JCPOA on our side and can go to the IAEA and our allies and explain why we need access, rather than if we give the impression that our objective is actually to force the Iranians into a crisis and blow up the regime.

Mr. FITZPATRICK. And is it your belief that Iran's ongoing support of regional proxies is not undermining the spirit of this agreement at best?

Mr. GORDON. Like I said, the agreement was to stop them from getting a nuclear weapon. I want to be absolutely clear that their support for proxies and terrorism in the region is something that should be an absolute priority of the United States to deal with, and there are ways of doing so consistent with the JCPOA. I would submit, respectfully, that not having the constraints on the nuclear program, unless we could also get every other American objective vis-a-vis Iran, could lead to us having neither. And that is why I think we need to deal with the proxies and support for terrorism, but it is a good thing to be constraining their nuclear program in the meantime.

Mr. FITZPATRICK. My time has expired. Madam Chair, I yield back.

Ms. ROS-LEHTINEN. Thank you, Mr. Fitzpatrick.

Mr. Boyle is recognized. And I want to say on behalf of Ambassador Wallace, a fellow "Cane," and I, we look forward to the University of Miami beating Notre Dame coming up pretty soon. [Laughter.]

Mr. BOYLE. Madam Chair, I regret that you just uttered fake news during this subcommittee, and I look forward to Notre Dame beating your alma mater. [Laughter.]

Mr. CONNOLLY. That would be huge. [Laughter.]

Mr. BOYLE. Thank you. Thank you, Madam Chair.

Actually, my line of questioning or commentary probably segues nicely from what Dr. Gordon was last saying. One of the criticisms or shortcomings that I saw in the JCPOA was that it didn't address Iranian funding of terrorism, its funding of Hezbollah, its involvement in Syria, what it is doing to support Hamas, et cetera.

Now advocates of the JCPOA pointed out that, well, wait a minute, that is not what it was designed to do; this is just dealing with the narrow issue of the nuclear program and that, outside the JCPOA, nothing prevented Congress from acting in those areas.

Once we signed up to the JCPOA with the international community, and it took effect, we moved forward in this committee on a pretty strong bipartisan basis, and in Congress on a strong bipartisan basis, and passed pretty strict sanctions this summer to do exactly that. So, to now revisit the JCPOA a couple of years after the date on which it went into effect, after we have already released approximately $115 billion, I am not sure what advantage we get out of that at this point in time.

Also, when keeping in mind that the Iranian issue is not the only issue out there, that in my view the single most important foreign policy issue we are dealing with at the moment is North Korea, I am not sure how it helps our efforts to negotiate North Korea away from developing its nuclear program if at the same time we are abrogating an agreement we made on a nuclear program with Iran.

So, given all of that, and as we are wrestling with this here in the United States and in the Capitol, those of us who were not enthusiastic of the deal or those of us who were mixed, I am curious what the view is in Europe. President Macron in France made a statement that he saw shortcomings in the JCPOA, especially with the sunsets, and wanted to work on that. But there has obviously been no enthusiasm for the approach that President Trump has singled out with unilaterally pulling out of the deal. So, I am wondering if any of you could comment on what the view is in Berlin, Paris, et cetera.

Mr. GORDON. I would be happy to start and let them speak for themselves. Only hours after the President's statement, the leaders of Britain, France, and Germany—May, Macron, and Merkel—put out a very strong and clear statement that they took note of the President's decision; they were concerned, which is not a word that they use often about U.S. foreign policy steps, they were concerned about the potential implications of decertification, and they remained fully committed to the deal, which they thought was working.

So, that doesn't mean it is wrong to say that Europeans have concerns about certain aspects of it, are willing to work with us on issues beyond the JCPOA, including terrorism, ballistic missiles, and they are, and we should follow up on that. But they have been absolutely clear that, having participated in these difficult 2-year negotiations with all the different parties, they know that you can't just revisit that in the way you said, Congressman, and just ask for those issues to be unilaterally revised.

So, that is why I said earlier in my remarks I think it is wishful thinking to imagine that we can amend, fix, or change this deal. Can we look at other ways to deal with issues that were not in the deal? Absolutely, and we should. But I think Europeans have been absolutely clear, and that is why I think it is a dangerous path we have headed down because, if the President's standard really is get Congress and the allies to change the deal or he will "terminate" it, then I think we are in trouble.

Mr. BOYLE. I will just say in the brief time I have left, I was very concerned myself or disturbed by a quote the German Foreign Minister gave to a German newspaper that, essentially, President Trump's behavior over the Iran deal "will drive us Europeans into a common position with Russia and China against the USA." I am wondering if we are seeing any sign of that happening.

Ambassador WALLACE. I don't think so. I think there are, obviously, some real concerns in a bipartisan manner and on the international stage about confusion in American policy. I don't speak for the administration. I said I don't want to; I am not going to. And I think that that is a problem.

We have seen definitely some signs out of Europe. Look, the Europeans are smart; they are sophisticated; they are concerned about Iran. There are some big business interests in Germany that they have longstanding business interests. The French, I don't want to speak for them. I have interactions with a lot of these governments. But I think the French are very clear-eyed in the concerns about some of the shortcomings of the deal, about perhaps using the leverage that we could have or gain to have supplemental or additional concerns.

But, more importantly to the French, I think, and I think something that we need to think about, is, how do we use the levers of power that we have or can build through actions in this Congress, for example, to put pressure on Iran to roll back Iran in other areas of its activities. I think that there is coalition waiting to be built in that area, in my opinion.

Mr. GORDON. Can I just add briefly? We are alone on this right now. I don't speak either for the Europeans or the Trump administration, but the Europeans have spoken for themselves. And that is the risk of this strategy. If they don't join us in following the President's demands, the United States, which was only successful on this issue because we got our international partners onboard— I mean, you know, the United States has had bilateral sanctions on Iran for decades.

Mr. BOYLE. Since 1979.

Mr. GORDON. I am sorry?

Mr. BOYLE. Since 1979.

Mr. GORDON. We don't trade with Iran. We don't invest in Iran. We don't have an Ambassador in Iran. And we saw the results of those sanctions, all too limited, especially where the nuclear program grew and grew, even when we had sanctions on. They became effective when we started to get international support, and Congress had a lot to do with that. And we brought Europeans together. And then, miraculously, we even got Russians and the Chinese and, as I mentioned on my testimony, India, South Korea, Japan, everyone to agree on a focused issue, which is stopping the Iranian nuclear program. And that is a fantastic position for the United States to be in when we need that leverage. The risk with this approach, I fear, is that we throw it away and we become the issue. The issue is not Iranian compliance; the issue is American compliance.

Ambassador WALLACE. If I may, the notion that our sanctions were effective from 1979 for decades is wrong. Our sanctions were not enforced, somewhat feckless. If you look at the chart of one of my colleagues who put up the chart, when this Congress, this committee, became engaged, and others became engaged, an active Treasury Department, and truly put on really effective sanctions, and tested the theory that sanctions could be effective and certain types of governments were vulnerable, it had a profound effect on the Iranian economy.

And I think all of us can agree that at least that, in part, drove Iran to the table because they were feeling financial pressure. We can debate about how much financial pressure they were feeling; I think a lot, and I think some of my colleagues in the previous administration would differ slightly. I think they would all agree that they were feeling some pressure.

But those sanctions were effective. I think we have to get back to the place in this Congress where all of you, or most of you, join together to put together a sanctions plan that ever increased pressure and drove economic indicators during the time periods that are shown in these charts.

Mr. BOYLE. Thank you, Madam Chair.

Ms. ROS-LEHTINEN. Thank you, Mr. Boyle. Go Canes.

And now, I am so pleased to recognize Mr. Kinzinger, and thank you for your service, as I always say.

Mr. KINZINGER. Thank you. Thank you, Madam Chair.

And thank you all for being here and taking some time with us today.

I will get back to this issue. I do want to say on the front end, just because it is apropos to what was just being discussed, sometimes leadership starts with standing alone, standing by yourself. I think if we decertify this deal, there are all kinds of questions of what happens. I think there is no question of what happens in 10 years, even if we certify this deal over and over again, which is we either have to basically bomb Iran to keep them from getting nuclear weapons or they are going to get nuclear weapons, or we have to somehow come back to the table and compel them to yet another nuclear deal.

It was actually pretty interesting and pretty eye-opening. Jake Sullivan, a couple of weeks ago, was in front of the committee, and I asked him, did you guys put ballistic missiles on the table in your opening gambit of this attempt to get a deal? And he said, yes, absolutely, but we knew the Iranians would never agree to it, so we pulled it off.

So, that actually reminded me of my thought that—and I think I said this to Secretary Kerry, or somebody before us, which is, you are going to get a deal at any cost. Because the Secretary was saying, "We're willing to walk away from the table." No, they weren't. The Obama administration was not going to walk away from the table and they would give in whatever they needed to give in order to get a deal, including saying that, hey, in 10 or 15 years this thing is off the table and we are going to be back to nukes. So, if we look at 100-year line of history from today to 100 years from now, a 10-year freeze on a nuclear program is cool for the next 10 years, but after the 10 years, so year 11 to 90, it doesn't make sense. This is the issue we are dealing with North Korea, too. How do you, when you give somebody the ability to go nuclear, how do you ever enforce a nonproliferation treaty?

The other point that was made is about Europe. Look, I have a lot of respect for Europe. I am a big believer in using multilateral approaches. I am not a unilateralist. But, at the same time, Europe has been rushing for the economic benefits of the Iran deal. So, this idea that Europe is somehow just genuinely concerned, maybe to an extent, but there is also a business reason for that. And that included, when we leveraged sanctions against Russia. They were resistant to that, despite Russian invasion of Crimea, Russian occupation of Georgia, and the continued fight in Eastern Europe, because it is about the economy.

For the entire panel, though, I am going to shift. I was horrified this week to see the images of a 1-month-old baby starving to death in Syria. What we have in Syria is one of the largest human tragedies, at least in my lifetime, hopefully, in my lifetime. Five hundred thousand dead people, 500,000 innocent children.

So, in addition to supporting Assad's barbarism, Iran is more emboldened in its efforts to dominate Syria and its efforts to build a regional land bridge. And I can only conclude that they are going, if successful, to use that to threaten Israel and other allies we have.

We didn't do enough or really anything in the last 8 years to sound the alarm on Iran's destabilizing activities in Syria and Iraq, I might add, of which I fought against them in Iraq, of which I also need to remind people that about a quarter of American soldiers that gave their life in Iraq were the result of Iran or Iranian technology. But I think now is the time to finally implement a broad strategy that counters Iran effectively in Syria.

Mr. Ambassador, I will start with you, but it is a question for all three of you. No one should have to see those images of starving children caused by an Iranian-backed Assad regime anymore. I also met with a survivor of torture in Assad's prison. As he was bawling to me and recounted some of the stuff that I think the devil himself would look at and go, "Man, I couldn't even have come up with anything that twisted." As he recounted this stuff to me, I realized this is like the shame of our generation to ignore what has been going on. But what specific pressure can we apply to the Iranians, be it sanctions or actual military engagement, to have an impact toward slowing their advance across the entire country, Mr. Ambassador?

Ambassador WALLACE. Look, I agree with a lot of what you said, probably all of it. The reality is that Iran—in politics today in Washington we oversell things. With due respect to my colleagues in the previous administration, one of the points of oversell—and, look, I get it; it is just the way it is here now—was that they said, somehow President Obama on implementation day said that Iran would rejoin the community of nations. I am paraphrasing. I don't remember the quote exactly.

But what Iran did, that wasn't true. It didn't work out that way. I believe that President Obama genuinely believed that. I believe he was wrong about that. Iran ran right to Damascus and right to Moscow. And look, for a country that complained about the horrific chemical attacks that Iran suffered at one point, and now, very comfortably, are allowing their proxy Assad to do it to his own people, I think speaks volumes about their lack of sincerity about building off the nuclear agreement to whatever term, you know, rejoin the community of nations.

So, I think what you propose, and I think what we are hearing, I hope is a bipartisan consensus, is that we have to push them back and we have to say to them that, if you are going to have militias there, if you are going to have your proxies there, we are going to continue to ratchet up pressure and do things and potentially take action against those proxies. If they stay there, we are not going to allow you to have, for example, that land bridge. We are not going to allow you to have the Bab-el-Mandeb. We are not going to allow that to happen. We want to avoid any military action, of course, and we should use our economic pressure and our leverage.

I believe that our coalition, there is a coalition out there, actually. But I do also believe that the 2008 financial crisis showed that, regrettably, or favorably in this case, that most of the international banking transactions and financial transactions flow through New York, and we have a lot of power to control that. Let's use our leverage. Let's use things that aren't bullets and bombs, at least to the first point, to try to stop Iran and push them back. Your points about pushing them back are dead on, sir.

Mr. KINZINGER. Thank you. And I am sorry the other two I won't, because I am overtime, but I appreciate you guys being here. And thank you for your time.

And I will yield back.

Ms. ROS-LEHTINEN. And thank you for your leadership on always calling attention to the crisis in Syria. The humanitarian toll is beyond comprehension.

Mr. Connolly of Virginia.

Mr. CONNOLLY. Thank you, Madam Chairman, and thank you for bringing this panel together.

I don't know that there is bipartisan consensus, Ambassador Wallace. I am not asking you a question. I am reacting to what you said. I take a fundamentally different approach. I support the JCPOA. Its goal was quite focused on one thing, pushing Iran back from the nuclear threshold as a nuclear threshold state. Estimates were they were within a year or so.

Dr. Gordon, how far away are they now?

Mr. GORDON. Now they are at least a year away, and at the time they were even less than a year, 2 or 3 months.

Mr. CONNOLLY. Well, but, Dr. Heinonen—and I assume that is a Finnish name?

Mr. HEINONEN. Yes, that is correct.

Mr. CONNOLLY. Kiitos [speaking in Finnish].

There were metrics set in JCPOA: Enriched uranium down to 3.68, I think. Have they met that goal, yes or no?

Mr. HEINONEN. The IAEA assessed that they are verifying and monitoring the Iranian—or the JCPOA. The IAEA has not explicitly provided the numbers there. They have given that story, the amount of uranium hexafluoride pure which is there.

Mr. CONNOLLY. But we do know that——

Mr. HEINONEN. But, for example, they have not given the amount of such material which is in place in Iran.

Mr. CONNOLLY. Well, my understanding from international sources is they have pretty much met the metrics set on enriched uranium and shipping it out of the country to Russia, as was indicated.

Centrifuges, they have reduced the number of centrifuges to the level specified in the agreement. The plutonium production reactor, they have cemented it over, as was required in the agreement. They have allowed the inspection of nuclear facilities, to my knowledge, unimpeded. Is that correct, Dr. Gordon, or have they, in fact, impeded some of those inspections?

Mr. GORDON. They have not——

Mr. CONNOLLY. We are arguing over non-nuclear, or we think non-nuclear, military facilities, and that is an argument worth hav- ing.

Now, Dr. Gordon, historically, when John Kennedy proposed the Nuclear Test Ban Treaty to try to prevent both the Soviet Union and the United States from open-air testing of nuclear weapons, did he insist that all other objectionable Soviet behavior be included before we signed that agreement?

Mr. GORDON. No, he did not.

Mr. CONNOLLY. I am sorry?

Mr. GORDON. No, he did not and——

Mr. CONNOLLY. When Henry Kissinger and Richard Nixon negotiated the SALT I agreement, did they insist that all negative behavior on the part of the Soviet Union, or objectionable behavior on the part of the Soviet Union, be incorporated into that agreement?

Mr. GORDON. They did not.

Mr. CONNOLLY. Salt II?

Mr. GORDON. No.

Mr. CONNOLLY. Why would that be?

Mr. GORDON. Because it would have been unrealistic to achieve all of those goals and——

Mr. CONNOLLY. Has there ever been a comprehensive, all-inclusive behavioral agreement between two nations or a multilateral entity and a nation that you are aware of historically?

Mr. GORDON. Not that I can think of, no.

Mr. CONNOLLY. No. So, we are dealing with a red herring.

When my friends on the other side of the aisle, who never supported JCPOA and who believed that, or certainly said that, in fact, approving the agreement would accelerate Iran's move toward a nuclear threshold state, and therefore, the agreement itself, as Benjamin Netanyahu said before a Joint Session of this Congress, uninvited by the Chief Executive of the country, nonetheless here, that actually approving the agreement would be an existential threat to Israel. I would propound that, actually, the existential threat to Israel is less on a nuclear basis today than it was when he gave that speech. What is the difference? The approval of the JCPOA.

Dr. Gordon?

Mr. GORDON. I will say one thing on that, because you brought up both the Iraq heavy water reactor and Israel, and we have some friends from Israel here with us today. As I mentioned in my written testimony, I recall quite vividly in 2013 meeting with Israel national security officials who were deeply worried about the completion, the scheduled completion of the heavy water reactor, because once live, it could produce enough plutonium for one or two weapons per year. That reactor is now dismantled and its core is filled with concrete, and the Israelis don't have to worry about the fissile material that, by now, would have accumulated to the point if we didn't have the deal——

Mr. CONNOLLY. Right.

Mr. GORDON [continuing]. For six nuclear weapons.

Mr. CONNOLLY. So, my time is almost up. But I fear this administration and the decision by the President not to certify, and some of the criticisms still being echoed here as if nothing had happened, as if there were no implementation metrics, is going to talk ourselves right out of a nuclear agreement that is working, not perfect, not permanent. We can work toward that. And we will damage the credibility of the United States that hosted this agreement. Remember, our adversaries as well as our allies were part of this agreement. We will never get Russia and China to the table again if we renounce this agreement, nor will we ever convince Iran that it is worth dealing with the United States on these or other issues, the very ones enunciated by my friends on the other side of the aisle.

If you want to make any progress at all—and I take Ambassador Wallace's statement to heart—don't overpromise. Don't overpromise. But to denigrate this agreement as if it hadn't achieved something quite fundamental, quite important as a building block, to me, is a disservice to the agreement, and it is going to talk ourselves right into a nuclear Iran when we are facing the nuclear threat from North Korea.

I yield back.

Ms. Ros-Lehtinen. Mr. Connolly, before I acknowledge your yielding back, Dr. Heinonen had put his hand up. I am wondering——

Mr. Connolly. Oh, I am sorry, Dr. Heinonen. I didn't see you. Thank you, Madam Chairman.

Mr. Heinonen. Thank you, Madam.

And, sir, I have a little bit different view with regard to the capabilities of the JCPOA. We have to look at any timeframe and a longer timeframe. It is true, as you said, that the so-called breakout time has now shortened. It is less than 10 years—sorry—less than 1 year. It is not actually past the 1-year mark, if you take all those items which I mentioned in my written statement.

But I think where we need to focus now is this sunset clause after years 10, 8 and 10, how to face the situation when Iran starts steadily to go closer and closer to this breakout capability, which will be much, much less than 1 year. I recall even President Obama saying somewhere year 12 or 13. It is a question of weeks. And I think this is what the people try to look at now, which kind of measures can be taken, perhaps without abandoning the agreement? But that is now measures to make sure that the deal forfeits its long-term goal, which is to deny from Iran access to nuclear weapons.

And a tiny, small clarification.

Mr. Connolly. Dr. Heinonen, sir——

Mr. Heinonen. Did you know, sir, that there is highly enriched uranium in Iran today? It is of U.S. origin, spent fuel in the Tehran research reactor. The JCPOA says that Iran intends to ship it out. I think we should encourage them to ship it out.

Mr. Connolly. Yes. Dr. Heinonen, I want to just respond real briefly. I agree with you that we have got to deal with those sunset provisions, but how do you deal with it? Let me just say to you, my experience in life is, when you threaten somebody, having already reached an agreement, and saying, we have changed our minds, we want to change the terms, we are going to renounce that, and now we are going to make you do it forever, the incentive for the other party to agree to that is quite limited, especially when it knows that our credibility is now so damaged that reinstating a sanctions regime with international cooperation is probably not going to happen.

And so, I think you have got to build on what we have built on to get the sunset provisions addressed. I fully agree with you. But how we do it matters a lot.

I yield back.

Ms. Ros-Lehtinen. Thank you very much, Mr. Connolly.

And I am so pleased to yield to my friend from Missouri, the Ambassador Ann Wagner.

Ms. Wagner. Thank you, Madam Chairman, for holding this hearing today.

The Iran nuclear deal, as Ambassador Wallace wrote, does not prevent a nuclear Iran. And as Dr. Heinonen wrote, the time to fix the deal is now, not 6 years from now when the deal's sunset clauses have helped Iran establish itself as a permanent threshold nuclear state.

I believe that Iran's centrifuge R&D program is an example of Iranian cheating on the deal. And I am also concerned that the IAEA continues to face access issues on the ground.

Dr. Gordon, you argue that sanctions relief has not fueled Iranian expansion in the Middle East. My understanding is that the $1.7 billion that the Obama administration paid to Iran during the 2016 ransom scandal were funneled straight into Iran's defense budget. I believe I read that in the FDD, the Foundation for Defense of Democracies' report on Tehran's budget.

Can you, or others on the panel, briefly explain if this was the case? And if it is the case, I don't understand how this money won't be used to destabilize the Middle East. Sir?

Mr. GORDON. Sure. Thank you.

Money is, of course, fungible. And so, I don't think there is any precise way of saying $1 went to one thing or another went to another. Clearly, if Iran is receiving money or having access to its frozen assets or able to sell oil, it gets more money and it can use it for nefarious purposes, which is a problem. I think everybody would agree that more fungible money for Iran to use for these purposes is a bad thing. I don't think, though, we can say there is some direct link to any particular asset that Iran has access to and its funding for these sorts of——

Ms. WAGNER. It is still $1.7 billion that they have used.

Mr. GORDON. That is correct, and Iran has a budget of tens of billions of dollars.

Ms. WAGNER. Thank you, Doctor. Thank you, Dr. Gordon.

Dr. Heinonen, you drew attention to Iranian Foreign Minister Javad Zarif, his comment that Iran will emerge from the nuclear deal with a stronger nuclear program. But I didn't see any comment in your statement about your opinion on the administration's decision not to certify the nuclear agreement. I am eager to hear your thoughts, especially in light of your study of the Iran regime's intentions. Sir?

Mr. HEINONEN. I didn't take any position to decertification. It is not in my domain. I am looking at the implementation of the JCPOA. Does it meet the requirements that it denies Iran's access to nuclear weapons in the short term and in the longer term? In the short term we are slightly better off in terms of the verification, but there are still important loopholes which need to be fixed in order to make it solid. It doesn't mean that you need to throw the agreement away. There might be ways and means to do some complementary measures.

But the issue is the long term. It is a very unique situation. We have here a country which has been in noncompliance with its Safeguards Agreements. The IAEA has not even yet concluded that Iran is in compliance. Let's not forget about it.

They are maintaining a sensitive nuclear program, uranium enrichment, with no technical economical reason. And as you quoted, Mr. Zarif is correct. After 8 years they will start to emerge from this with much more powerful centrifuges.

Ms. WAGNER. Right.

Mr. HEINONEN. And at the same time, there is no limitation for their missile program. So, in my view, we face a situation which needs fixing.

Ms. WAGNER. It needs fixing.

Mr. HEINONEN. The time to do is now.

Ms. WAGNER. Thank you.

Mr. HEINONEN. And I refer to North Korea. I was watching while the people were rating what happens in North Korea. Now we see where we are today.

Ms. WAGNER. On the same path.

Thank you very much.

Ambassador Wallace, I am eager to hear your perspective on when Congress should reimpose snapback sanctions. Your written statement did encourage Congress to pass legislation that reaffirms congressional willingness to reimpose sanctions if the deal is not strengthened.

Ambassador WALLACE. I think that the starting point is what we all learned. This committee really became the expert. We all learned that, if you continue to apply pressure with Iran knowing, and the business interests around the world knowing, that pressure would increase thereafter if compliance wasn't better, I think that is the strategic posture that this committee has to be in.

And for lack of a better term, an unfortunate one, it is a target-rich environment when it comes to sanctioning Iran. There are lots of things you can sanction them for. I do believe there is no reason for them to have a ballistic missile program. Their ballistic missile program is to carry nuclear weapons. It is not part of the agreement, but I don't think any reasonable person could say that long-range ballistic missiles with the warheads that they have—are designed ultimately for nuclear weapons.

So, I think you start with things like designating the Quds Force. I think this committee should start examining their behavior and pushing them back, strictly enforcing the agreement. And when they engage in a violation, it is not a technical violation; it is a violation, and we should indicate that we are willing to impose sanctions if they do.

Ms. WAGNER. Absolutely. A violation is a violation. The time to fix the deal is now, not 6 years from now.

I thank you very much for all your testimony.

Thank you, Madam Chair, for your indulgence.

Ms. ROS-LEHTINEN. Thank you so much, Ambassador.

And now, I am pleased to yield to the ranking member, Mr. Deutch, for his closing remarks and questions.

Mr. DEUTCH. I thank the chairman.

I want to go back to Ambassador Wallace's initial comments about you, Madam Chairman, only to say that I think what happened here today is really an excellent representation of the way that you have conducted this committee. This was an important hearing on a critical issue with excellent witnesses, serious discussion, and very little political grandstanding. This is the way that we need to address, I would suggest, all issues in Congress, but it is absolutely true with respect to Iran.

I would also suggest that, if you listened really carefully today, really carefully, you recognize that there is a consensus. There is a consensus. Dr. Heinonen talked about ways to get access to military sites that currently exist within the deal, and I would like to explore that in a minute. Dr. Gordon talked about increasing international pressure on Iran's malign activity, consistent with the JCPOA and working with our allies. Ambassador Wallace talked about meeting the challenge of Iranian hegemony. There is, as I said in my opening comments, strong bipartisan support to do all of that. And that is the moment that we find ourselves in.

But the only comment I would make about the JCPOA and snap-back sanctions, and throwing out the deal and the threat to walk away from the deal, is those very concerns that we have about the sunset provisions that are legitimate, that I share, we are worried about what will happen after 10 years. If we walk away from the deal, those sunset provisions go from 10 years to tomorrow.

So, I think we need to find ways to recognize this bipartisan commitment to focusing on what Iran is doing, because what Iran is doing right now is an immediate threat to our nation and to our allies. And so, there will be lots of additional discussion about the JCPOA, and I know how strongly people feel about it, but we cannot allow the rehashing of all of the pros and cons of the JCPOA to interfere with our need to go after what I thought was best summed up on the chart that shows Iranian influence spreading throughout the region.

And Representative Kinzinger is right, and he knows better than anyone, as someone who faced the fire in battle with Iranian support and Iranian munitions that were responsible for killing American soldiers. He understands the need to take seriously what that map shows, Iran's efforts to expand its influence throughout, its support for terror throughout the region and throughout the world. It is horrific human rights violations.

And as, again, my friend Mr. Kinzinger referred to, the fact that it is Iran's support that has helped Assad slaughter ½ million people. And wherever you are politically in this country, it is impossible to not find that appalling and shocking, and recognize it as one of the worst human rights abuses in modern history.

So, given all of that, I thank the witnesses for a really important discussion. And I hope that we have the opportunity to continue moving forward now.

Dr. Heinonen talked about access to the military sites. Dr. Gordon, the JCPOA provides a means to get access, correct?

Mr. GORDON. Correct.

Mr. DEUTCH. So, Dr. Heinonen, there is a way. So, rather than all of the rhetoric that we have so often heard about how we haven't had access, isn't it appropriate for America to lead the effort with our allies under the JCPOA to get access to those military sites?

Mr. HEINONEN. [Mr. Heinonen looks up but does not verbally respond.]

Mr. DEUTCH. Yes, it is. I will continue. [Laughter.]

And when it comes to increasing sanctions on Iran, don't tell me that—I don't accept the Iranian argument that somehow increasing sanctions on Iran for everything that they are doing that is outside the deal violates the deal, when what we were told at the time by everyone involved was that the JCPOA was meant to address the nuclear program in Iran only.

And given that that is the case, and, Ambassador Wallace, I completely agree that we should be holding hearings in this committee—and I will talk to the chairman, and I am sure we will find ways to do it—about exactly what those—you have given a couple of ideas; there are lots of others out there. What steps can be taken, starting, by the way, with the legislation that Congress passed during the summer to impose sanctions on Iran, continuing with the legislation that the House is going to pass today to go after Iran's ballistic missile program? We ought to build on that. There is strong bipartisan support for that.

And finally, we ought to do exactly what Dr. Gordon says, which is find ways to increase international pressure consistent with the JCPOA and working with our allies. We ought to pursue the offer that we heard coming out of France to find ways outside of the deal to address the sunset clauses, to make clear what American policy is going forward.

There is not a lot that I find heartening these days in Congress. This morning's hearing is one such moment. I think there is a lot to build upon to strengthen the terms of the JCPOA without interfering with the relationship that we have with our allies; in fact, to help lead our allies. I think there is a way forward on additional sanctions to block Iran's territorial efforts and their efforts to expand influence throughout the region. I think it is possible to go forward and make sure that the IAEA is being as transparent as they should be and need to be under the deal.

And I am most grateful to you, Madam Chairman, for calling this hearing, and to our three excellent witnesses for giving us the opportunity to start to pursue these things.

Ms. ROS-LEHTINEN. Thank you so much, Mr. Deutch, and we all look forward to supporting your bill on the Floor today.

Thank you for excellent panelists, and thank you to our audience for being civil throughout. We appreciate it, to our friends in Code Pink.

Thank you.

And with that, the subcommittee is adjourned.

[Whereupon, at 12:04 p.m., the subcommittee was adjourned.]

A P P E N D I X

SUBCOMMITTEE HEARING NOTICE
COMMITTEE ON FOREIGN AFFAIRS
U.S. HOUSE OF REPRESENTATIVES
WASHINGTON, DC 20515-6128

Subcommittee on the Middle East and North Africa
Ileana Ros-Lehtinen (R-FL), Chairman

October 18, 2017

TO: MEMBERS OF THE COMMITTEE ON FOREIGN AFFAIRS

You are respectfully requested to attend an OPEN hearing of the Committee on Foreign Affairs to be held by the Subcommittee on the Middle East and North Africa in Room 2172 of the Rayburn House Office Building (and available live on the Committee website at http://www.ForeignAffairs.house.gov).

DATE: Wednesday, October 25, 2017

TIME: 10:00 a.m.

SUBJECT: The President's Iran Decision: Next Steps

WITNESSES: Olli Heinonen, Ph.D.
Senior Advisor on Science and Nonproliferation
Foundation for Defense of Democracies
(*Former Deputy Director General of the International Atomic Energy Agency*)

The Honorable Mark Wallace
Chief Executive Officer
United Against Nuclear Iran
(*Former U.S. Ambassador to the United Nations for Management and Reform*)

Philip H. Gordon, Ph.D.
Mary and David Boies Senior Fellow in U.S. Foreign Policy
Council on Foreign Relations
(*Former White House Director for the Middle East, North Africa, and the Gulf Region*)

By Direction of the Chairman

The Committee on Foreign Affairs seeks to make its facilities accessible to persons with disabilities. If you are in need of special accommodations, please call 202/225-5021 at least four business days in advance of the event, whenever practicable. Questions with regard to special accommodations in general (including availability of Committee materials in alternative formats and assistive listening devices) may be directed to the Committee.

COMMITTEE ON FOREIGN AFFAIRS

MINUTES OF SUBCOMMITTEE ON _______ *Middle East and North Africa* _______ HEARING

Day **_Wednesday_** Date _______ *10/25/17* _______ Room _______ *2172* _______

Starting Time _____ *10:05 AM* _____ Ending Time _____ *12:03 PM* _____

Recesses |____| (____ to ____) (____ to ____) (____ to ____) (____ to ____) (____ to ____) (____ to ____)

Presiding Member(s)

Chairman Ros-Lehtinen

Check all of the following that apply:

Open Session ✓
Executive (closed) Session ☐
Televised ✓

Electronically Recorded (taped) ✓
Stenographic Record ✓

TITLE OF HEARING:

The President's Iran Decision: Next Steps

SUBCOMMITTEE MEMBERS PRESENT:

GOP- Chairman Ros-Lehtinen, Reps. Chabot, Cook, DeSantis, Meadows, Kinzinger, Zeldin, Wagner, Mast, Fitzpatrick
Dem- Ranking Member Deutch, Reps. Connolly, Cicilline, Gabbard, Boyle, Schneider, Lieu

NON-SUBCOMMITTEE MEMBERS PRESENT: *(Mark with an * if they are not members of full committee.)*

GOP- Rep. Yoho

HEARING WITNESSES: Same as meeting notice attached? Yes ✓ No ☐
(If "no", please list below and include title, agency, department, or organization.)

STATEMENTS FOR THE RECORD: *(List any statements submitted for the record.)*

Representative Connolly's Statement for the Record

TIME SCHEDULED TO RECONVENE _______
or
TIME ADJOURNED _____ *12:03* _____

Subcommittee Staff Associate

Statement for the Record
Submitted by Mr. Connolly of Virginia

On October 13, President Trump declined to certify to Congress that Iran was complying with the Joint Comprehensive Plan of Action (JCPOA), despite lacking evidence of Iranian violations of the agreement. In the wake of the president's unfounded decision, I fear we are sleepwalking into an armed conflict. The hidden scandal of the Iraq War — the manipulation of intelligence to support a predetermined outcome — is now an overt political strategy to undermine a multilateral nonproliferation agreement. At a time when Iran was hurtling toward a nuclear threshold not easily undone by force or persuasion, the United States struck an accord with allies and adversaries alike that averted the solution everyone feared most — the kinetic option. Now, those most vocal prior to the deal about the imminent threat of a nuclear Iran want to scrap the deal, put the world back on the brink of conflict, and open up a second nuclear front.

By all accounts, Iran is in compliance with the JCPOA, and the deal is accomplishing a critical national security priority – preventing Iran from obtaining a nuclear weapon. Pursuant to the terms of the agreement, Iran has poured concrete into its plutonium reactor, reduced its centrifuges from 19,000 to 6,104, reduced its stockpile of enriched uranium to no more than 300 kilograms enriched no higher than 3.67 percent, and submitted to continuous monitoring and inspections at its key nuclear facilities. The International Atomic Energy Agency has released nine verification and monitoring reports indicating that Iran has not violated the agreement, and the President has certified to Congress six times that Iran is in compliance.

Critics of the JCPOA charge that it is not an all-encompassing agreement addressing all of Iran's malign behavior. Iran's repeated testing of ballistic missiles runs contrary to the United Nations Security Council Resolution 2231. Iran's Islamic Revolutionary Guard Corps (IRGC) continues to bankroll and arm regional terrorist organizations, including Hezbollah and Hamas, that threaten our greatest ally in the Middle East, Israel. Iran further acts as a destabilizing force in the region by supporting the Houthis in Yemen and Shia militias in Iraq and Syria. And on the home front, the Iranian regime engages in significant human rights abuses to maintain its brutal stranglehold on the Iranian people.

Each of these behaviors constitutes a threat to the United States and therefore demands an appropriate response. That is precisely why we recently enacted the Countering America's Adversaries Through Sanctions Act (P.L. 115-44), which is the most robust sanctions regime ever passed by Congress. If President Trump shares my concern for Iran's other destabilizing behavior, then he should employ the authorities granted him under that law, which the administration has failed to implement. Trump has no overarching strategy to counter Iran's behavior and his administration's unilateral retreat has left a vacuum in Syria. There are serious concerns that the Syrian de-escalation zones, negotiated by the Trump Administration and Russia, have allowed Iran to operate freely on Israel's border.

Trump's decision to decertify Iran's compliance with the agreement has reignited the previously contained threat of a nuclear Tehran. If Congress reimposes nuclear sanctions on Iran, violating U.S. commitments under the deal, it will enable that which we all can agree is an unacceptable outcome – a nuclear-armed Iran. Withdrawing from the JCPOA allows Iran to immediately restart its nuclear program, and leaves the United States with only military options to combat Iranian nuclear proliferation. The last thing the world needs right now is an additional nuclear front. In order to prevent such a dire result, Congress must work in concert with the Administration to ensure that the nuclear agreement is fully implemented and strictly enforced.

To this end, I have reintroduced bipartisan legislation with my Republican colleague Rep. Francis Rooney to establish a Congressional-Executive Commission to verify Iran's compliance with its obligations under the deal. The Commission to Verify Iranian Nuclear Compliance Act (H.R. 3810) would ensure close and enduring Congressional oversight of the JCPOA as well as coordination between Congress and the Administration regarding implementation of the deal. Congress should act immediately to advance one of the rare proposals on Capitol Hill that has garnered support from both sides of the heated JCPOA debate.

Withdrawing from the deal would damage U.S. credibility in the eyes of our allies and adversaries and weaken our leverage to negotiate future agreements with Iran or other states. The leaders of all parties to the deal, including many members of Trump's own administration, maintain that Iran is in compliance. Chairman of the Joint Chiefs of Staff General Joseph Dunford reiterated that "Iran is not in material breach of the agreement, and I do believe the agreement to date has delayed the development of a nuclear capability by Iran." Secretary of Defense Jim Mattis added that he believes it is in the U.S. national security interest to remain in the JCPOA. Furthermore, our partners are unwilling to return to the negotiating table. We should always endeavor to improve the deal and further constrain the Iranian nuclear program, but not in a unilateral fashion and not at the expense of the broader agreement.

The President's decertification without evidence is a nakedly political move with serious consequences for U.S. national security. This action has severely weakened U.S. leverage to avert a nuclear-armed Iran or to curb Iran's other abhorrent behavior. I look forward to hearing from our witnesses regarding how Congress can regain the trust of our P5+1 partners, ensure strict enforcement and transparency of the JCPOA, and apply lessons learned from that effort to the myriad threats posed by the Iranian regime.

www.ingramcontent.com/pod-product-compliance
Lightning Source LLC
Chambersburg PA
CBHW080902260726
48660CB00009B/3411